- AUG 2016

302.2314

Withdrawn From Stock
Dublin City Public Libraries

Blogging

D0309960

Withdrawn From Stock
Dublin City Public Libraries

Studies in New Media
Series Editor: John Allen Hendricks, Stephen F. Austin State University

This series aims to advance the theoretical and practical understanding of the emergence, adoption, and influence of new technologies. It provides a venue to explore how New Media technologies are changing the media landscape in the twenty-first century.

Titles in the Series

The Twenty-First-Century Media Industry: Economic and Managerial Implications in the Age of New Media, edited by John Allen Hendricks
Blogging: How Our Private Thoughts Went Public by Kristin Roeschenthaler Wolfe

Blogging

How Our Private Thoughts Went Public

Kristin Roeschenthaler Wolfe

LEXINGTON BOOKS
Lanham • Boulder • New York • Toronto • Plymouth, UK

Published by Lexington Books
A wholly owned subsidary of Rowman & Littlefield
4501 Forbes Boulevard, Suite 200, Lanham, Maryland 20706
www.rowman.com

16 Carlisle Street, London W1D 3BT, United Kingdom

Copyright © 2014 by Lexington Books

All rights reserved. No part of this book may be reproduced in any form or by any
electronic or mechanical means, including information storage and retrieval systems,
without written permission from the publisher, except by a reviewer who may quote
passages in a review.

British Library Cataloguing in Publication Information Available

Library of Congress Cataloging-in-Publication Data

**The hardback edition of this book was previously catalogued by the Library of Congress as
follows:**

ISBN 978-0-7391-8645-9 (cloth : alk. paper)
ISBN 978-0-7391-9804-9 (pbk. : alk. paper)
ISBN 978-0-7391-8646-6 (electronic)

Wolfe, Kristin Roeschenthaler, 1970-
Blogging : how our private thoughts went public / Kristin Roeschenthaler Wolfe.
pages cm. -- (Studies in new media)
Includes index.
1. Blogs. 2. Self-disclosure. I. Title.
TK5105.8884.W65 2014
302.23'14--dc23
2014012218

∞™ The paper used in this publication meets the minimum requirements of American
National Standard for Information Sciences Permanence of Paper for Printed Library
Materials, ANSI/NISO Z39.48-1992.

Printed in the United States of America

Thank you,
Don Wolfe, my wonderful husband, for supporting me through my PhD and this process and completely understanding the late nights and massive frustrations.

Bob and Laurenna Roeschenthaler, my parents, who always told me I could do anything, and allowed me try.

Dr. Calvin Troup for being my mentor and guide throughout this project.

Dr. Fadoua Loudiy for her friendship and for being my writing partner as I worked.

Dr. Adil Waheed, Dr. Srinivas Murali, and Dr. David Celko for getting, and keeping, me healthy enough to complete this project.

Alison Pavan, Emily Frazzette, Kathleen Bromelow, and everyone at Lexington books, for their assistance and guidance through the publication process.

John Allen Hendricks for including my work in your social media series.

Contents

1 Historical Journey from Diaries and Journals to Personal Blogs   1

2 Hannah Arendt's Understanding of Public, Private, and Social   19

3 Interpersonal Communication and the Role of Communication Technology   37

4 Personal Blogs: History, Usage, Future—Are We Just Looking for Our 15 Minutes of Fame?   55

5 Personal Blogs that Do More   71

6 Using Arendt to Navigate the Future of Communication Technology   79

Works Cited   91

Index   95

About the Author   97

Chapter One

Historical Journey from Diaries and Journals to Personal Blogs

As long as humans have been able to communicate, they have been passing down stories in order to share experiences and lessons learned. This is one way communities grow and people learn how to live together. Stories of great hunts and warriors were passed on by storytelling.

As far back as ancient Greece, people understood that they must examine their own life. Socrates said, "a life without investigation is not worth living" (Plato 24). Taking Socrates' observation to another level, Emerson realized that investigating is one step, but writing down events and feelings made it easier to examine and investigate life's challenges and successes (transcendentalism-legacy.tamu.edu/).

Not all things needed to be shared with the community; however, people wanted to be able to account for their life and share information with their children and their children's children. Why should future generations not learn from past mistakes and also learn something about their ancestors? Who does not want to leave their mark on the world, in some way? The various genres of self-representational writing provide a way for a person to be remembered. Anne Frank, for example, wrote her diary because she wanted to be remembered after her death (197). Writing down adventures, misadventures, and everyday happenings provides an accounting of a life, ensuring that a person would be remembered and their life would have made an impact, however small, on the future. There are many reasons people begin writing about their lives; however, one noteworthy reason is that people want to be remembered, they want to be immortal. The written word is one way to do that.

Andy Warhol's fifteen minutes of fame can be achieved through a written record of a life; whether the document was written to be private and only

Leabharlanna Poiblí Chathair Bhaile Átha Cliath
Dublin City Public Libraries

discovered after the writer's death, or the document was written with a specific audience in mind, one thing is certain: self-representational writing always provides a glimpse into a way of life, or an individual's life, that would not be accessible if someone had not taken the time to write down their thoughts, concerns, and activities. This written record provides the writer their proverbial fifteen minutes.

Virginia Woolf realized that the past urges us to leave a trace of our lives (Johnson 6). Aristotle wrote that man is a social animal and thank goodness for that, otherwise we would still be making the same mistakes as our ancestors because they would not have shared these details without storytelling and/or the written word (*Politics* 3). This trace, in the form of self-representational writing, allows the human race to evolve and grow in our communication habits and in our ability to live together in a community.

Examining the different genres of self-representational writing and their evolution throughout history allows us to examine the evolution of society in terms of the type of communication that is shared and the different levels of sharing that were, and are, considered acceptable or desirable at different times in human history. We begin with the diary, which is written as a private document for the future self, not to be shared with anyone until after the writer's death. Although many people still keep diaries, others wanted to hear opinions on life-changing situations, and self-representational writing began to be shared through journals. These writers know that they will have an audience; however, it will be limited to those whom the writer chooses, at least as long as the writer is still alive. The autobiography allows a person to write his or her life story with the knowledge that people, both known and unknown to the author, will read it to gain a glimpse into life as the writer perceived it. In the twentieth-century, technology evolved so that people could share self-representational writing on the Internet in the form of personal blogs. These writers not only know that there will be an audience of both people they know and people they might never meet, but they value the input and allow comments and feedback regarding their entries or posts.

This book focuses on the diary, journal, and personal blog specifically because of their similar formats. All three genres use a chronological format. All three provide a date at the top of the entry allowing the reader to follow the author's life as it occurs. Because of their similar formats, these types of self-representational writings allow for a compare and contrast examination of their communication styles. Utilizing the work of Hannah Arendt regarding public, private, and social we begin to study these forms of writing from a philosophical standpoint to further examine the extent of communicative sharing through self-representational writing.

Later, we will fully delve into Arendt's understanding of public, private, and social; for now we will summarize these terms as:

> Private: self or family
> Public: community
> Social: largely connected world of individuals.

These terms suggest that the diary belongs in the realm of the private; the journal in the realm of the public; and the blog also in the realm as of the public as we examine below.

DIARIES

It is best to start with a definition of the term diary. Diaries provide a way for writers to make connections between unspoken ideas in their mind, about remembering, and connecting these ideas to make sense of life. The connection that is described in this definition would be to connect events or ideas to each other and for the individual to understand how these things relate to each other in terms of his or her life. Since diaries are written for the author alone, the connections are not about connecting with other people, but about making connections between ideas and events the author experienced.

Why has the art of writing diaries lasted for so many generations? Why did people start writing diaries and why do they continue today? Steven Kagle, in his text *American Diary Literature 1620–1799*, explains that the diary is often "born of a tension, disequilibrium in the life of its author, which needs to be resolved or held in check. A journey, a new role, a spiritual crisis—these are some of the sources of tension that can bring about and sustain a diary" (17). This statement begins to examine why people write diaries. Although, today, many people believe that the diary is mostly a habit of females, history shows that many men have kept diaries. Some of the more famous include Samuel Pepys, Clerk of the Acts and Secretary to the Admiralty; John Adams and other members of the Adams family; Ralph Waldo Emerson; and Henry David Thoreau. Many other men kept diaries also; but the diaries of the men listed above have become part of the public record.[1]

Diaries help to clarify a specific situation in the mind of the diarist. By writing about something and rereading past entries, the individual may be able to better understand a situation that they are currently in. Writing things down always seems to shed light on a situation. By being able to review what was written, the diarist can take lessons learned from previous experiences and apply them to what is happening at any given time. This allows the diarist to avoid repeating the same actions over and over. Just as our ancestors' diaries help to share information so that we do not repeat their mistakes, rereading our own diary can keep us from repeating our own.

Although each diary is written in response to a life-changing situation, or a situation that the author is struggling with, there should be no limits on what is written in the diary; anything that affects the diarist and inspires them to write should be included. Limiting the diary to only a specific topic does not do the diary or the diarist any favors as something that seems completely unrelated to the topic may help to clarify a situation and, if the scope of writing is limited, it may be lost from the author's memory. A diary provides the writer a venue to record his or her life as his or her values may shift and the amount and type of knowledge that he or she gains may change (Kagle, *American* 15). This written record allows the writer to review this change and take note of the events and circumstances that brought it about, permitting the diarist to gain a better understanding of him- or herself. The diary is, therefore, an invaluable tool to help an individual grow and evolve throughout his or her life.

One of the advantages of writing a diary is the privacy and the freedom that comes from knowing that you are not writing for an audience. This freedom from criticism may lead to more honest writing. Anne Frank shares how this lack of audience affected her writing: "There is a saying that 'paper is more patient than man' . . . Yes, there is no doubt that paper is patient and as I don't intend to show this cardboard-covered notebook, bearing the proud name of 'diary,' to anyone" (2). Through this quote Frank begins to demonstrate a common feeling of many diarists—no one else would be interested in what I am writing. However, the popularity of the diary as literature demonstrates that people are interested in reading about ordinary people's lives. After all, Anne Frank was not famous until her father published her diary.

Diaries can only be expected to remain private as long as the author is alive. Kagle emphasizes the near impossibility to keep things private and the expectation of the diarist as to who will read his or her diary (*Early,* 6). There really is no such thing as eternal privacy. If something is written down, expect that someday someone will see it. This discussion leads into the research of journals—understood for our purposes as self-representational writing that was expected to be shared with select others whom the writer chose.

JOURNALS

The need to bring in another person or persons for an opinion may have led to a shift in the intent of self-representational writing. Although there are many people who still keep a private diary in which to share their thoughts and dreams with no one other than their future self, many people decided to share their journal with others to gain insight and input, possibly becoming momentarily famous to the readers of their journal.

The journal differs from the private diary mainly due to its focus of writing for an external audience. Kagle explains, "even those diarists who have claimed to be writing for themselves, even those who would profess horror at the idea that anyone else might see their 'private confessions' have been writing for an audience" (*Early,* 5). Kagle's point is well taken; a writer must have someone in mind whom they are writing for. Take a moment and try to write something with no audience, including yourself, in mind. It is almost impossible, right? Without a notion of audience, the tone and word choice is extremely difficult to select; therefore, on some level, every diarist or journal-writer has someone in mind as they write.

The writers of journals in early nineteenth-century America had discovered the literary value of diaries and, therefore, decided to make their writings public. Because the writers in the early nineteenth century read the private diaries of others, they were aware that their writings would likely become public also. This shift in the degree of privacy that a person hoped to keep begins to demonstrate that people realized there was a limit to keeping something private forever. This tradition of sharing self-representational writing also occurred in the salons that took place in Europe pre-World War II. The salons allowed people of different classes and genders to come together to share in conversation and ideas. Many of the "conversation starters" may have come from a journal entry even though the other participants were not made aware of this connection.

Another important movement in the historic shift from private diary to public journal was Transcendentalism.[2] The Transcendentalists' journals demonstrated two emerging characteristics in American journals: "extreme-length and self-conscious literary intent" (Kagle, *American* 183). These journals were kept by many famous writers including Ralph Waldo Emerson and Henry David Thoreau. By writing in their journals, these men and women could more easily evaluate their ideas for future inventions or literary endeavors.

Sharing their journal with close friends and family became popular with authors and others who wanted input into either their writing style or a complex situation that they needed help with. This sharing of his or her writing led the author to be conscious of perception and response as the author wrote. This consciousness likely led to editing and careful word choice on the part of the writer. When the author assumed his or her writing would remain private, proper grammar and spelling would not have been deemed as important. Now, however, the author did not want to appear uneducated because of his or her writing. Kagle explains that the journals of the early nineteenth century differ from the diaries of the seventeenth and eighteenth centuries in language and in the variety of topics written about. One reason was the "result of the influence of the sophisticated culture of the urban centers" (Kagle, *Early* 1). Many factors influence the grammatical content of a journal because the author must now consider the perception of the public to his or her writing.

The knowledge of an audience may also have influenced the type of information that was shared. One example was the journal of Amos Bronson Alcott. Alcott showed his journal to many of his friends who were also writers, including Emerson, Thoreau, and Fuller, claiming that his journal was his confessional. He shared his journal with his wife, who took issue with the content if it involved her. "Alcott protested that he had only written from his 'convictions and what seemed . . . plain fact,' she placed some of these passages 'under the ban of her scissors,' removing them from the manuscript (2/2/39)" (Kagle, *Early* 129). Alcott showed no reservations in sharing his deepest thoughts and feelings with those he considered close friends and family; however, his wife obviously had issues with appearing in a bad light, hence her editing. Public perception and response definitely played a role in Alcott's journal content.

The possibility of an audience provided a focus of sorts to the journal. A private diary would not need to be as clear to someone else, as long as the diarist understood the entry. Now, with the focus on another, the journal must be written more coherently. An excellent example of this audience consciousness can be seen in the journal kept by Lewis and Clark. Most of their journals captured descriptions of the landscape and information that would be essential as others began to move westward. Therefore, the journal of Lewis and Clark was one of the most important instruments they carried (Kagle, *Early* 31).

Another change to self-representational writing brought on by an audience was the desire to provide some biographical information about the author. This can be seen in Richard Henry Dana, Jr.'s writing. Dana knew that all or part of his journal would become public so he provided an autobiographical section prefacing it by writing that no author "could help but think about an audience or avoid subjectivity . . ." (Kagle, *Late* 66). This example demonstrates that many journal-writers understood that someone, at some time, would read their journal. This knowledge of an audience led some, like Dana, to provide more information about themselves than would need to be shared in a private diary.

Writing their journal for an audience also provided benefits to professional writers, or those who hoped to become professional writers—it allowed them a venue to hone their craft. Emerson and other American Transcendentalists wrote in their journals "as a means of improving their writing and as a sourcebook that might be mined for materials to be used in their public writings" (Kagle, *Early* 104). Accessing story ideas through reading one's journal became common for many authors at this time. "It was in his [Thoreau's] journals that the moment of inspiration was captured for later revision" into *Walden* (Kagle, *American* 184). As this example demonstrates, journal writers had come to realize not only the possibility of someone reading their journal, but also the benefits of journal writing to the creative process.

Emerson used his journal to improve his writing because "he mistrusted his ability." The journal gave Emerson a way to "experiment with his technique" and "express his strongest feelings." Much of what Emerson published was considered "outspoken" but Kagle points out "he [Emerson] 'sometimes toned down or altered his original thought when he presented it for public consumption' (1:xxxii)" (*Early* 107). Journals sparked ideas and provided training for some of the greatest authors to create great works of literature.

Revision of journal entries played a key role in utilizing real life experiences to include in literature. Kagle explained that comparing the original journal entry and the revisions allowed an observer to see how the work changed as the anticipated audience changed (*Early,* 6). An author must write and revise for an audience, no matter who or what that audience is, especially if the work is to be published.

Writing itself takes on a public or private aspect and the author cannot change that. Once something is written down it is never completely and eternally private; once something is written down expect that someday someone will see it. This statement was true when things were written with pen and paper; it becomes more accurate in the age of computers. Once a file is saved on a computer, unless the computer is properly wiped clean, someone will be able to find that file. Once a document, post, or comment is placed on the Internet, it is available forever. This raises the question—why do so many people place self-representational writing on the Internet in the form of a personal blog? Why are people allowing others—friends, family, and even total strangers—to read their writing?

BLOGS

The Origins of Blogging

Before examining the origin of the weblog, let us examine the history of the World Wide Web. In 1990, Tim Berners-Lee's boss approved his "global hypertext system." Berners-Lee called his project "World Wide Web." Berners-Lee wanted to build a system that was "equal parts readable and writable—the latter part of his genius was essentially forgotten until blogging came along" (Stone 12). Without his vision, there would be no World Wide Web, and there would be no blogging. His vision took nine years to come to realization with the introduction of the weblog, but Berners-Lee created a way for people to write, read, and respond to each other no matter where they were located.

This technology would change the way that humans lived, learned, and communicated. Suddenly, a lot of information, some accurate and some not, was available with just a couple of clicks of a mouse or some typing on a keyboard. A benefit to making information very accessible, which most people can agree on, is that people can communicate with others around the world. Whether it be to conduct business, strike up a friendship, start a romantic relationship, find lost friends and relatives, or make new friends, the World Wide Web can assist with any and all of these endeavors. As the Web grew from offices to homes across America and then around the world, millions of people were theoretically able to publish their thoughts for millions of other people to read. "The Web implicitly invited people to say anything and everything" (Rosenberg 11). Blogging has made it possible for people to share their opinions and thoughts freely. There was finally a place that freedom of speech knew no bounds—we didn't need a lot of money to publish our words, just a connection to the Internet, and a thought. The obvious exclusions to this include libel and slander (Bick 43–45). Say what you want about yourself and others, as long as it is accurate and not malicious; however, remember that nothing on the Internet is private. Anything you post on the Internet can be viewed by anyone who has Internet access, although many people feel protected by the sheer size of the Internet.

One of the major drawbacks of the Internet is the ability to overshare. Justin Hall invented oversharing—the desire to tell anyone everything about your life—from his dorm room in 1994 (Rosenberg 17). Some researchers and readers commonly call personal blogs "what I had for lunch" sites; because bloggers may feel the need to be current and post regularly, some may list what they ate for lunch or dinner, or what they wore to work or school.

What is Blogging?

> Is blogging self-expression, personal publishing, a diary, amateur journalism, the biggest disruptive technology since e-mail, an online community, alternative media, curriculum for students, a customer relations strategy, knowledge management, navel gazing, a solution to boredom, a dream job, a style of writing, e-mail to everyone, a fad, an answer to illiteracy, an online persona, social networking, resume fodder, phonecam pictures, or something to hide from your mother? It's all of those things and more. (Stone 34–35)

Blogs began as a way for technology enthusiasts to share links to other websites with each other. These types of sites can be traced back to 1994 with the start of Justin Hall's *Links from the Underground* (Stone 37). Besides sharing hyperlinks, the main commonality of these early blogs and the personal blogs of today is the fact that all entries are listed with the most recent one at the top of the page, making it easy for readers to find the newest information shared on the website. The technology enthusiasts realized there was a market for software that would allow others, who were not as adept at writing computer code, to utilize this type of website. This led to a flood of blogging software released in 1999 and 2000. Such software included Blogger, Movable Type, and Live Journal, to name a few that still exist today (Stone 38; Serfaty 20). This software allowed anyone who wanted to start a blog to be able to do so. And so, blogging became a new mass medium. Blogging is communicating at its global finest, utilizing the Internet in all its communication glory.

Although blogging had taken hold in 1999 and 2000, it truly came into the public eye in 2001 with the terrorist attacks on September 11. Traditional media could not keep up with the events, and many bloggers were giving eyewitness accounts of the attacks (Stone 38). This onslaught of blogging entries and newsworthy updates regarding such a horrific situation brought blogging into the foreground of mainstream society. "In retrospect, 9/11 hardly marked any sort of maturity for blogging. Instead, it marked the moment that the rest of the media woke up and noticed what the Web had birthed" (Rosenberg 8). The number of blogs continues to grow, even today with social networking sites becoming mainstream, and it is the ability to write and receive feedback almost instantly that makes blogging a mainstay.

"The blog is a new rhetorical opportunity, made possible by technology that is becoming more available and easier to use, but it was adopted so quickly and widely that it must be serving some well-established rhetorical needs" (Miller and Shepherd). Obviously, blogs filled a void in terms of communication and rhetoric. Through the ability to share ideas, opinions, and daily life experiences with many people at once, the personal blog provided a one-to-many channel similar to, but not as intrusive as, email. This ability to share personal ideas with the masses and not need an editor, who may edit the opinion, provided a way for an individual to share his or her thoughts as the person so chose.

This rhetorical opportunity to speak one's mind without censorship provided a communication channel that allowed freedom of speech to take on a greater meaning to the common person. "The cultural moment in which the blog appeared is a *kairos* that has shifted the boundary between the public and the private and the relationship between the mediated and unmediated experience" (Miller and Shepherd). People had ideas to share and information to communicate, but they were not sure how to do this efficiently; along came the blogging software which opened the floodgates for individuals to share their knowledge and opinions with others, including those outside of their usual social circle. The ability to share with others, including those outside of the expected social circle, allows bloggers to expand, not only the reach of their interests, but also the ability to learn new things and meet new people.

Blogs began to become a form of mainstream communication during the 1990s. An examination of society during this time period demonstrates that people were sharing more information with anyone who would listen than at any other time in history. Such cultural events included the Clinton-Lewinsky scandal and the introduction of reality television. These events helped to establish the blog and its rhetorical qualities as a specific genre (Miller and Shepherd). Blogging has similarities to many of its predecessors, but it is a creation of the Internet and therefore, although the similarities are there, blogs are truly unique in their format and reach combined. Technological availability is what made blogging happen. According to Miller and Shepherd, the technology allowed the blog to encompass "the diary, the clipping service, the broadside, the anthology, the commonplace book, the ship's log."

The timing of the technological advancement, the 1990s, could not have been more perfect based on cultural events. By combining different elements of the services listed above, blogging allowed people to share links, news, and opinions in a way that made it easy for readers to find the newest information and for those readers to comment on the posts shared. Taking the best of each of the genres listed above, the personal blog allows the bloggers to share links (the clipping service), share personal anecdotes (the diary), announce events and information to many people at once (the broadside), discuss many topics in one location (the anthology), share phrases and quotations (the commonplace book), and keep a record of the blogger's activities in one location (the ship's log). By combining these aspects of existing written genres, the personal blog allows a person to keep track of his or her life and receive input and comments on any activities that he or she chooses to share.

Blogging is about sharing and discussing information, it is not a one-way channel; bloggers hope to engage in conversation about their posts. Blogging is a two-way communication channel in which bloggers and readers have the ability to engage in a dialogue about whatever is on their minds. Blogs are dialogues between the author and his/her readers and his-/herself. "[T]he blogging ethos—shared by Hall and Winer and Sippey and Barger and all the other early weblog enthusiasts who would soon follow their lead—was different. These under-the-radar upstarts said, 'Here are things that are of interest to *me*. Maybe you'll like them too'" (Rosenberg 85).

The blogosphere is a community, albeit a virtual one, of real relationships, and it grows every day. An example of the reality of these relationships can be seen in a personal interview with Liberty, a blogger since 1999 who blogs at colorfully-see-through-head.com. She explained this community dynamic when describing a time that she posted about losing her Christmas decorations. Liberty explained that she used her blog to work through her disappointment but that "within days, packages from all over the country started pouring in. I even received packages from Canada and eventually Australia with Christmas ornaments to replace those I had lost." More than twenty people, many of whom she did not know, sent ornaments to Liberty. "Without my blog, that miracle never would have happened, certainly not on that kind of scale" (Personal Interview 2006). Through the reach of the blogosphere and the relationships that are created, Liberty's Christmas, and that of her family, was made brighter because of her blog readers. If taking care of each other through difficult situations does not demonstrate "real" relationships, what does? Relationships are about caring for the other person; this example demonstrates that bloggers do care about each other on more than a superficial level.

Why People Blog

People decide to start blogging for many reasons including: all of their friends have blogs; they want to share their story; they want to share information or learn more about something; they want to be remembered after they are gone; etc. Wanting to share their story and wanting to be remembered are two ways in which blogging is similar to past self-representational writing genres. Blogging provides an avenue for a person to do research and learn more about a subject which interests the blogger (Stone 115). By providing and sharing information, blogging helps people to gain knowledge and learn from each other. It also allows the blogger to write, think, and search on a regular basis; thus allowing the blogger to become smarter (Stone 115). Nardi et al. provide five motivations for blogging that were discovered during their research: "documenting one's life; providing commentary and opinions; expressing deeply felt emotions; articulating ideas through writing; and forming and maintaining community forums" (43). Sharing information and communicating on a regular basis allows the blogger to obtain a greater knowledgebase on topics that are of interest to him or her and find a way to coherently explain the information to his or her readers.

Blogging is storytelling, and most of the stories are about real life. "37% of bloggers cite 'my life and experiences' as a primary topic of their blog" (Lenhart and Fox). Storytelling is yet another way that blogs and previous self-representational genres are similar. Self-representational writing tells the story of the author's life and blogs do something very similar. After all, storytelling is how people share experiences with each other and with future generations. Arendt explained:

> . . . every individual life between birth and death can eventually be told as a story with beginning and end is the prepolitical and prehistorical condition of

history, the great story without beginning and end. But the reason why each human life tells its story and why history ultimately becomes the storybook of mankind, with many actors and speakers and yet without any tangible authors, is that both are the outcome of action (*Human* 184).

The storyteller then provides the experience to future generations. The actor may complete the task, but the storyteller documents it for others. The blogger knows that it is important to read others' blogs as a way to truly understand the community that is the blogosphere. "Blogging is as much about reading other blogs as about writing your own, and the best way to understand blogging is to immerse yourself in it." (Walker Rettberg 1)

Of course, many times, in terms of self-representational writing, the actor and the storyteller are one and the same. Reading and writing are a part of the blogosphere, and this demonstrates Aristotle's insistence that man is a social animal (*Politics* 3). The need and desire to communicate with others is what sets man apart from all other animals. This desire is fueled by the fire of the Internet and blogging as it opens up the communication to many more people than traditional communication outlets allow. According to Parks and Floyd, "computer-mediated communication liberates interpersonal relations from the confines of physical locality and thus creates opportunities for new, but genuine, personal relationships and communities (e.g., Pool, 1983; Rheingold, 1993)" (81). By providing a way for people to communicate with others around the globe, the Internet allows the world to seem like a much smaller place as people can communicate with anyone, anywhere.

Blogging embodies a return to an oral culture in many ways; because blogs are conversational and very social they are able to change their tone and be less formal, resembling everyday speech instead of traditional written language (Walker Rettberg 33). By allowing information to be edited after it is published and by using a more conversational tone than traditional written media, blogs bring us back to a simpler way of communicating. Walker Rettberg explains, "[o]ur transition from print to electronic media has been characterized by the scholar Walter Ong as a *secondary orality*, a return in some ways to a culture more like that of the Ancient Greeks than of the post-Gutenberg society (Ong 1982)" (33).

Echoing the ancient marketplace, the electronic marketplace allows for stories to be told and retold, sometimes with information changing with each retelling. The information in the stories can be passed on to those not currently at the marketplace through retelling of the story; similarly, bloggers can repost a story they read somewhere, or they can simply link to the original post, allowing others who may not have seen the original post to read the information as well. Blogs are not written in a formal, grammatically correct style, but are written as if the blogger were speaking to the audience, using contractions, slang, and all the other idiosyncrasies of the spoken language.

This accessibility of language allows for a wider audience to understand and share the blog post.

Blogs allow for dialogue between blogger and readers and also between readers and other readers. Because most blogs allow for the ability of others to comment on a post, it provides a way to disagree with or to clarify the original remark. If the reader does not understand what the blogger is trying to say, the comments section provides a way to start a dialogue to clarify the original post; it is even possible that another commenter may clarify the post better, or before, the blogger has an opportunity. Also, the comments section provides a way to create dialogue and discussion if a reader does not agree with what the blogger posted. This can lead to an interesting thread as others may, and usually will, join in the conversation to either clarify a side of the argument, choose a side of the argument, or just to provide their own opinion. Dialogue "points to a particular relationally based process/quality of communication in which the participants not only meet to exchange messages but to allow fully for changing and being changed" (Anderson et al. 92–93). If the blogger were not open to discussion and the possibility of a change in his or her opinion, more than likely he or she would not have posted to the blog or allowed for comments. The ability of a one-to-many communication, such as the blog post, can lead to a many-to-many communication as commenters and the blogger alike have the ability to communicate about the topic at hand.

Arguments that suggest that dialogue must be face to face need to be addressed. According to Anderson et al., "[a]lthough Bakhtin did not focus on electronic media, he showed through his analysis of fiction that the technology of writing is yet another avenue to dialogue" (103). After all, according to Plato, writing was not rhetoric, only the spoken word was true rhetoric. That communication form has been revisited and acknowledged as a form of rhetoric in today's society. Is it not time to revisit the meaning of dialogue to include computer-mediated avenues?

Blogging is participatory. Blogging allows for two-way communication between the blogger and the commenter or reader. It is important to "define the difference between public and audience. An audience is passive; a public is participatory" (Perseus Publishing Editors 9). Bloggers are not looking for an audience, they are looking for a public. Most, if not all, bloggers allow for comments on their posts because the blogger is looking for feedback. Most bloggers do not hope that all of their readers agree with them all of the time; many are looking for a forum to argue their case and prove the validity of their ideas. However, feedback and many readers is not the norm for most blogs. In fact Rosenberg explains that most bloggers are famous for fifteen people (90). Because the Web is so vast, it is often difficult to garner a lot of traffic to a personal blog so instead of Warhol's fifteen minutes of fame, Web insiders began to comment that bloggers were famous, not for fifteen minutes, but only for fifteen people.

A blog is merely a message board if no one responds to the posts. Bloggers and blog readers build traffic and community through the give and take of communication. It is not a one-way forum for the blogger to spout his or her opinion, but a rhetorical space for the interaction of ideas and opinions. Many modern philosophers believe that the new electronic environment is a move toward "increased presence and rejuvenated possibilities for dialogue" (Anderson et al. 106). Blogging is one way that dialogue can be achieved in a technological environment.

How honest are the bloggers in what they share on their blog? Most bloggers will admit that they do not share every minute detail of their lives on their blog, but only those things that they want an opinion on or that they are interested in learning more about. Many bloggers share details to the point that regular or frequent readers often feel like they know the blogger personally. It is difficult to read someone's personal writings for a period of time and not begin to feel like you know the author. Bloggers cannot stop their personality from coming through in their day-to-day writings, especially since many blogs are about everyday events, which makes the readers of the blog feel like they know the author. Whether the blogger is someone whom the reader already knew or someone who had opinions and/or stories that interested that person, there is a community feeling that grows among the blogger and readers. Many bloggers meet in person after reading each others' blogs for a while, taking the virtual relationship into a real-world relationship.

Blogging allows people to share their true feelings about events happening around them. Many times people will not stop and say that there is a problem with something, but a blog allows them to do that. Matt Welch, a Los Angeles-based writer, began a blog one week after 9/11. "'Starting a blog,' Welch says, 'was a chance to stand up to people I'd walked among for fifteen years and yell ENOUGH!'" (Rosenberg 138). The ability to state his opinion without interruption or argument, at least until he stated his full opinion, allowed Welch, and many other bloggers, to express his true thoughts on a given situation.

The first personal blog was started by Justin Hall when he was a freshman at Swarthmore College (Stefanac 50). Hall wrote with an honesty and audacity unheard of when he started. Reading any personal blog over a period of time, even a week, gives the reader a glimpse into who the blogger truly is. It is difficult to completely hide behind the screen and eventually the person behind the blog begins to peek through and reveal him- or herself to the readers.

Because the blogger puts the information "out there," he or she is hoping for someone to see the information or photos that are available. Bloggers believe that they can hid behind the screen while sharing their innermost thoughts and feelings without worrying about identification or humiliation and believe that they can go undetected while observing others (Serfaty 13). This interest in sharing details with others willingly is indicative of the "me" culture. Blogging allows the author to shout "look at me" without physically causing a scene, but still attracting the desired attention.

Blogs provide a way for the blogger to share information with distant friends and family, as well as make new friends along the way. A benefit of blogging is that it combines "the immediacy of up-to-the-minute posts, latest first, with a strong sense of the author's personality, passions, and point of view" (Nardi et al. 42). Knowing the blogger is a feeling that separates visitors of a blog from those of someone who hosts a personal webpage. Not always will the writer's true personality come through on a webpage, but it is difficult for a blogger to hide behind the screen indefinitely.

However dissimilar, most bloggers have personal codes of ethics dictating what goes into their blogs. An example of this type of code comes from a post by Beth Fish on her blog, http://www.sothefishsaid.com, on August 24, 2007: "I am shocked, positively shocked, by the number of you who claimed you were unaware that we had boundaries. People, there is so much that I don't tell you, and I can assure you that we are all much happier that way." Beth set up a set of guidelines for herself regarding what she would and would not blog about; these codes of ethics vary from blogger to blogger. The code of ethics created by the blogger can evolve over time as the person continues to blog and the blog continues to evolve in the blogosphere.

If the intent of the blog is to share information with people the blogger already knows, many wonder why the blogger does not just send an email. The reason, Nardi et al., discovered was that "blogs are not intrusive. No one is 'forced to pay attention,' observed Lara, as they are with email. Reading is voluntary, when convenient" (43). People find a need to read email when it appears and also feel the need to respond; with a personal blog, reading feels more voluntary and commenting even more so. Blogs allow people who want to find out what someone is doing the ability to do so without feeling the *need* to stay up to date.

Public vs. Private in Blogs

As previously addressed, once something is written down there is little hope of it staying private forever. Blogging, however, takes this issue to a whole new level. Gunter refers to a paper by Gillian Youngs that "examines the public versus private spheres of blogging and identifies that in blogging the 'public' can become personal and the 'private' becomes public" (124). This leads to a blurring of the two areas of society and an opportunity to engage in a study of Hannah Arendt's public, private, and social spheres in terms of the twenty-first century and the new technologies that are available to us.

Why Study Blogs?

With the growth of social media, such as Facebook, Twitter, and Google+, why should anyone pay attention to research regarding blogs? Blogs are the original social media. It is of utmost importance to study the beginning of a genre, especially when that beginning product is still used and remains an impressive force in the social media universe.

Although the growth of new blogs has slowed, and the genre has been almost abandoned by the younger generation, the use of blogging has remained a constant among those over twenty-five. The true benefit of a blog is the "power it bestows upon its owner" (Stone 36). This power to share ideas and have a voice allows bloggers to participate in public and social discussions, demonstrating a greater democratic forum. Applying Arendt's philosophy regarding private, public, and social to twenty-first century technology such as personal blogging allows us to examine interpersonal communication and its evolution through the history of mankind.

SUMMARY

All three genres of self-representational writing we have examined—the diary, the journal, and the blog—are still used today; therefore, a distinction must be reiterated explaining both the connection and divergence among these genres. It is especially important to examine how each genre is affected by the perceived audience; as well as how Arendt's understanding of public, private, and social may be applied.

A brief review reminds us that the diary is not expected to be read by anyone other than the writer until after his or her death. The journal is expected to be viewed by those select individuals that the writer deems appropriate. The personal blog is accessible to anyone who has access to the World Wide Web making the audience immeasurable. The diary, therefore, represents the private; the journal, the public; and the blog falls in line with the public, also. This determination is based on the anticipated audience for each type of self-representational writing that determines what is written and how it is written. The diarist does not feel the need to correct every grammatical or spelling error because the expected audience is only a future self, thus falling into the private sphere. The journal writer must take into account spelling, grammar, and word choice because close friends and family will be reading their journal; however, an error here or there will usually be overlooked; the blogger must pay very close attention to word choice, spelling, and grammar because anyone can read his or her posts and without a personal relationship with the blogger, the mistake may be seen as something larger than a typographical error. The need to keep the audience engaged and entertained is one major difference between the diary and the blog. Since the diarist is writing for a future self as his or her primary audience, the diarist does not have as much pressure to keep the diary updated daily with interesting details. The blogger, however, must attempt to keep an audience engaged, and that involves regular and interesting posts.

Finding a way to keep the audience engaged and entertained is a large difference between previous self-representational genres and the personal blog. Keeping the audience entertained involves posting on a regular basis and posting something of interest to the blog's readers. The diarist is writing for his or her future self as the primary audience; therefore, the diarist does not have as much pressure to keep the diary updated daily with interesting details.

By engaging Hannah Arendt's philosophy to distinguish these genres, this study hopes to provide a clearer delineation of each genre and also demonstrate a greater understanding of each sphere and the related genre. Arendt's view of private as for the self, or family, falls in line with the diary. Her view of public as being community directly relates to the specific, limited audience who is exposed to the journal. Finally, the super-human family that Arendt expresses as the social can be related to the reach of the World Wide Web on which blogs are published. Although the technology did not exist for the World Wide Web when Arendt was alive, her foresight into what technology could do lends her thinking to be engaged to study personal blogging.

NOTES

1. This information was obtained from Steven Kagle's books *American Diary Literature 1620–1799*; *Early Nineteenth-Century American Diary Literature*; and *Late Nineteenth-Century American Diary Literature*.

2. For more information regarding Transcendetalism visit http://www.emersoncentral.com/transcendentalist.htm.

Chapter Two

Hannah Arendt's Understanding of Public, Private, and Social

How can the work of a philosopher who died fifteen years before the advent of the World Wide Web provide any insight into the study of personal blogs? Using Hannah Arendt's work on public, private, and social will enable this research to clearly delineate self-representational writing into these realms and provide a historical look at how communication has evolved.

> The distinction between the private and the public sphere of life corresponds to the household and the political realms, which have existed as distinct, separate entities at least since the rise of the ancient city-state, but the emergence of the social realm, which is neither private nor public, strictly speaking, is a relatively new phenomenon whose origin coincided with the emergence of the modern age and which found its political form in the nation-state (Arendt, *Human* 28).

Arendt's distinction is grounded in Aristotle's understanding of the *polis* and *oikos*. One major difference between the two was that the *polis* knew only equals but the household, or *oikos*, was the center of inequality (Arendt, *Human* 32). The *polis* in Ancient Greece included only property owners in the city-state.

The definitions of public, private, and social evolved throughout history. Grounding these terms in a philosophical tradition, such as the philosophy of Hannah Arendt, demonstrates the changes in their definitions and the ever-fluid understanding of communication; thus allowing us to examine how self-representational writing went from something not to be shared to something to be shared with the world at large. Why do people feel that something so extremely personal that at one point in history it was kept under lock and key can now be shared on the World Wide Web for all who wish to read it?

Through Arendt's philosophy of the public and social and her clarification of the blurring of the public and private that the rise of the social has brought about, this study hopes to provide a better communicative map of what is consistently referred to as "oversharing."

This discussion begins with the different understandings of the public and private communities. Farrell explains that throughout the years the differences between public and private has reversed many times. At one point moral character and integrity were related to the public while the private was tied to creativity and imagination. Today morals have become private and aesthetics are tied mostly to the public (Farrell 150). Arendt, relying on Aristotle, saw the public as being more than political life. She believed that humans do not have an "essence" the way that other things do but that "who" a human being is can be disclosed only through action, which takes place in the public sphere (Øverenget 430). A closer examination of these terms will help to further clarify the terms' etymology.

Arendt develops her understanding of the public and private realms simultaneously. Arendt noted that:

> The true character of this *polis* is still quite manifest in Plato's and Aristotle's political philosophies, even if the borderline between household and *polis* is occasionally blurred, especially in Plato who, probably following Socrates, began to draw his examples and illustrations for the *polis* from everyday experiences in private life, but also in Aristotle when he, following Plato, tentatively assumed that at least the historical origin of the *polis* must be connected with the necessities of life and that only its content or inherent aim (*telos*) transcends life in the "good life." *(Human 37)*

This "good life" is a term that Aristotle coined to describe "the life of the citizen." In *The Human Condition* Arendt elaborates that the "good life" is not better or more carefree than any other type of life, but is a different quality of life. Aristotle considered it the "good life" because the individual had all of the necessities of life taken care of and was therefore not a slave to biological processes *(Human 36–37)*. The "good life" was the life one lived after the basic necessities of living were achieved.

PRIVATE

According to the ancients, private life meant that the person was "not fully human" (Arendt, *Human*, 38). Because humans are social animals, they need to be with others in order to be completely human and a private life would not allow that. The evolution of the term private includes the Greeks believing that private life was "idiotic"; the Romans believing that privacy was only a temporary break from the public world; and today where privacy is more closely related to intimacy that was "unknown to any period prior to the modern age" (Arendt, *Human* 38). This description furthers Arendt's definition of the private.

Plato's attempt to arrange the public as an extended form of the private begins an examination of a concept of the social that had yet to be addressed or even considered. Arendt describes the social realm as a "super-human family," referring to Plato's suggestion of how to manage or rule the *polis* in the best possible way for all citizens.

Moving through history, Arendt also addresses the understanding of the public and private realms after the fall of the Roman Empire. She equates the public to the religious and the private to anything related to the secular realm (*Human* 34). The prominence of the Catholic Church in this era brought about such a major shift in these definitions as the faithful became more concerned with life after death than the life they were living.

Arendt continues that the Medieval mindset which brought all human activity into the private realm extended into Medieval professional organizations such as the "guilds, *confréries*, and *compagnons*, and even into the early business companies where the original joint household would seem to be indicated by the very word 'company' (*companis*)" (*Human* 34–35). In Medieval times the "common good" only meant that individuals have interests in common, whether they are material or spiritual, and that in order to handle most of their lives privately they must also be aware of and protective of the common. This distinction from the Ancients can be demonstrated by showing that the political was public—or part of the *polis*—for the Ancients, but private—or part of the secular—in Medieval times.

From the Middle Ages, Arendt moves into the sixteenth century with the work of Jean-Jacques Rousseau regarding intimacy. Arendt describes Rousseau as "the first articulate explorer and to an extent even theorist of intimacy . . . who, characteristically enough, is the only great author still frequently cited by his first name alone" (*Human* 38–39). This intimacy that Rousseau refers to is a replacement of the private at this point in history. Arendt explains that "the intimacy of the heart, unlike the private household, has no objective tangible place in the world, nor can the society against which it protests and asserts itself be localized with the same certainty as the public space" (*Human* 39). She addresses the dichotomy of Rousseau's thinking by suggesting that the intimate and social were subjective to Rousseau's way of thinking. This dichotomy points to the inner struggle of humans to want to be a part of society, but at the same time to want to rebel against it. This struggle continues today in many people and began with the rise of the social out of the private and public.

Today, privacy refers to the intimate rather than the family. And, according to Arendt, "under modern circumstances, this deprivation of 'objective' relationships to others and of a reality guaranteed through them has become the mass phenomenon of loneliness, where it has assumed its most extreme and most antihuman form" (*Human* 58–59). Privacy, in the modern world, has become a problem of isolation rather than the safety of the household. However, the private can be seen as the ability to keep some information and experiences either known only to the individual or to the individual and those few that he or she deems worthy to share the information with. In this manner, privacy becomes more of a privilege than a burden or a misfortune. The private means that something is so important to the individual that he or she does not want to share it or that he or she only wants to share it with those people that are truly important. This evolution of the private realm can best be seen in a comparison with the evolution of the public realm, which is examined next.

PUBLIC

> The public is where human beings interact for the good of the community or *polis*. Being seen and being heard by others derive their significance from the fact that everybody sees and hears from a different position. This is the meaning of public life, compared to which even the richest and most satisfying family life can offer only the prolongation or multiplication of one's own position with its attending aspects and perspectives. . . . Only where things can be seen by many in a variety of aspects without changing their identity, so that those who are gathered around them know they see sameness in utter diversity, can worldly reality truly and reliably appear. (Arendt, *Human* 57)

The public allows those experiences that must be observed by others to exist and become reality. By closely examining the evolution of the public realm from Ancient Greece to the present day, we can begin to see how the public has, in some ways, expanded in its definition.

According to Arendt, the public "does not always exist" and most men "do not live in it" (*Human* 199). This statement refers strictly to the political understanding of public. However, many people would not be allowed to or would not want to participate in this aspect of a shared realm.

The only consistent feature of the public realm, throughout history, deals with the concept of living with others outside of the household. "Human beings are plural and mortal, and it is these features of the human condition that give politics both its miraculous openness and its desperate contingency" (Arendt, *Human* xvii). This plurality helps to explain why human beings live in communities and not in isolation from each other.

In Ancient Greece, the *polis* or public realm was defined as the city-state; however, Arendt clarifies that the *polis* did not mean the physical location but the interaction of the people through acting and speaking with each other. The location is not as important as the people to the *polis*. The public is the space where we appear to one another. This begins to clarify the *polis* in terms of citizens and location. The connection of the *polis* and the household rests in mastering the necessities of life. The *polis* was freedom from these necessities in order to be involved in politics (Arendt, *Human* 29–30). In order for a citizen to be involved in politics, one must first have truly understood and cared for the basic necessities of life: food, shelter, and safety. Only then was man able to focus on the *polis*. However, in order to participate in the *polis*, a man must own land (Arendt, *Human* 29–30). This kept slaves and foreigners from having a say in the activities and governing of the *polis*.

Although the *polis* provided freedom, it also provided competition. This competition revolved around finding a way to stand out and distinguish himself from everyone else; to be an individual. Distinguishing himself allowed the citizen to create an identity separate from the household. Arendt explains:

> Every activity performed in public can attain an excellence never matched in privacy; for excellence, by definition, the presence of others is always required, and this presence needs the formality of the public, constituted by one's peers, it cannot be the casual, familiar presence of one's equals or inferiors. (*Human* 48–49)

Competition brings out both the best and the worst in men. This need for recognition causes harm and hostility in the *polis*. However, the public realm was also the space in which an individual could gain immortal fame for his uniqueness. This distinctness was easier to establish away from the household and the fame that could be achieved needed to be observed by more than just household members.

This recognition leading to immortality needed to exist in public so that future generations could learn about the person's achievements and share them with others. It is because of this that storytelling becomes important for Arendt and for the ability to learn from the past and engage in thoughts of the future. The *polis*, therefore, allows the stories of the Greeks and Romans to be shared to the present day and helps to shape each shared or public space in history and in the future.

Arendt valued storytelling because it focused on the nature of human experience more so than philosophy did. In *The Human Condition* she demonstrates her belief that storytellers are very important to anyone's life being remembered. According to Arendt, without storytelling, Achilles, Hercules, and Perseus would remain mortal men whose bravery and conquests would be forgotten. Storytelling did not disappear with the Ancients but continued into the Middle Ages, also.

In Medieval times, the public realm was specifically tied to the church—more accurately, Christianity. The public, things that would be seen by others, included only activities involving the church and charitable actions. The main concern with the public realm, in terms of Christianity had to do with a "good" deed being done for God. In Medieval times people addressed the need to replace the political with something else to help the community. "The medieval concept of the 'common good,' far from indicating the existence of a political realm recognizes only that private individuals have interests in common, material and spiritual, and that they can retain their privacy and attend to their own business only if one of them takes it upon himself to look out for this common interest" (Arendt, *Human*, 35). This common good was charity.

Augustine believed that, on some level, all members of humanity had a form of charity inside of them that could be used to assist the community. This "common good" of charity allowed the public to take a new form in Medieval times. Arendt explains that the Medieval concept of the common good "recognizes only that private individuals have interests in common, material and spiritual, and that they can retain their privacy and attend to their own business only if one of them takes it upon himself to look out for this common interest" (*Human* 35). By realizing that the common good must be addressed in order for individual life to flourish, the Medieval man took the necessary steps to address the public aspect of charity.

Many stories from Medieval times were written as poetry to recount tales of greatness and ordinary life. It was the length and memorability of the poem which make it the genre of choice. This storytelling through poetry allowed those in Medieval times to recall events.

Arendt's examination of the early modern era demonstrates the need to share information with selected confidantes through salons and also demonstrates the economical and marketplace aspects of the public realm. Arendt wrote a book on Rahel Varnhagen based on the letters and diaries that she left behind. Three thinkers—Adam Smith, Karl Marx, and Rahel Varnhagen—provide Arendt with a political, as well as philosophical, examination of this time period. Addressing the changes, in chronological order, will build upon the understanding of the public realm as we approach modernity and the present day.

Arendt believed that money and public admiration, or the need for greatness as defined in ancient times, became equal substitutes for each other at this time. The modern thought regarding the public realm was expressed when Adam Smith stated that "men of letters" recognized the importance of public admiration, as well as monetary compensation, in terms of professional success (Arendt, *Human* 56). Both of these needs, Arendt explains, are necessary for life in the public realm and in the world at large. Food is necessary for life itself, and public admiration is necessary for self-worth in the public realm no matter why the person is admired.

Arendt considers the public realm as equal to the marketplace and not the politics of a given community. This distinction demonstrates the beginning of the evolution of the public realm from something that was strictly a political arena into something more which many Arendtian scholars believe comes closer to her interpretation of the public. This something more is the marketplace. The marketplace was the place where craftsmen would gather to sell their products and catch up on current events. This understanding of the public does not discount the political in the public realm, but only enlarges the understanding of the public to include areas other than the political.

Arendt enlarges her sense of the public realm beyond the political in her discussions of the salons that emerged during the German Enlightenment. Rahel Varnhagen was a Jewish woman during the late 1700s hundreds into the early to mid 1800s hundreds and was an outcast or "pariah" in her time because, although her father was rich, when he died he left her nothing. As time went on, Rahel became the center of salons in Germany which brought great minds and individuals together for intellectual discussion. The salons at this time provided a social area outside of society to discuss ideas and current events. Rahel's salons brought people from many different ways of life together in order to discuss current affairs and other important topics in a public arena.

"Rahel shared her thoughts so freely with those in her circle that she told Viet that he could share her letters because she felt it might make people understand her better" (Arendt, *Rahel* 19). This statement illuminates the growth of the public realm to include things that past generations would have considered to be private. However, it demonstrates some control as only those that Veit knew would possibly have access to her documents. Although the public and private began to blur during this time, there was still some control over the visibility of communication.

Rahel's salons provided much comfort to those who wished to discuss different topics no matter what their social status was. Rahel's salons were a place where class did not matter and each person was considered only as an individual. In her salons "private things were given objectivity by being communicated, and in which public matters counted only insofar as they had private significance—this salon ceased to exist when the public world, the power of general misfortune, became so overwhelming that it could no longer be translated into private terms" (Arendt, *Rahel* 122). This ended the salons in Germany and other parts of the world and began a time of political struggle for much of the world.

This political struggle involved Karl Marx and his ascent into the economic and political spotlight. Marx recognized the natural distinction of workers and facilitators. He understood that it took different types or classes of people to keep mankind moving forward, in addition to the fact that work value and social value were of great importance to communities. Values are never the product of one human, but are determined by the interaction and the exchanges of members of society. "Nobody, as Marx rightly insisted, seen 'in his isolation produces values,' and nobody, he could have added, in his isolation cares about them" (Arendt, *Human* 164–165). Marx's view of value was the amount of work and time put into a product, and not the community's desire for the product. In other words, if one item took four hours to construct, it should hold the same value as any other item that took four hours to create. This view of value does not take into account supply and demand, but specific utility. This utility allowed all work to be valued based on the quality of the product, allowing the craftsman to be appreciated in the public realm for the product he produced. Marx's comments need to be understood within the early manifestation of modernity, which was Arendt's primary concern.

Modernity brings us into the Industrial Revolution and beyond, moving into the Machine Age. The first and most relevant change to the public realm, at this time, is the exclusion of the political from the public. This exclusion was an attempt to focus on production and consumption as opposed to political discussion and lack of action. What this meant for the political man was that there was a move to a more social realm as Arendt explained because the larger the population, as was true of the modern age, the more likely that politics would become a product of the social realm and move away from the public (*Human* 43). This shift of the political will be examined more closely later in the chapter.

Another relevant change in the public realm was the inclusion of labor and the labor class. Labor, to Arendt, has a different connotation than work. Relying on her understanding of Marx's philosophy, she notes:

> Labor was to him the "reproduction of one's own life" which assured the survival of the individual, and begetting was the production "of foreign life" which assured the survival of the species. This insight is chronologically the never-forgotten origin of his theory, which he then elaborated by substituting for "abstract labor" the labor power of a living organism and by understanding labor's surplus that amount of labor power still extant after the means for the laborer's own reproduction have been produced. (*Human* 106)

The "reproduction of one's own life" prior to the modern age would be considered part of the private, as it was a function of the household. This inclusion significantly affected the future of the world. For Arendt, the admission of labor into the public has "transformed it into a swiftly progressing development whose results have in a few centuries totally changed the whole inhabited world" (*Human* 47). By bringing labor into the public realm, the community saw what was happening in terms of the amount of labor being completed and the conditions under which the laborers were forced to work. This admission helped to improve labor conditions and establish the first national labor union in 1866 (aflcio). The introduction of labor into the public realm also brought action into the public realm.

Action does not always mean work, but is not possible in isolation or privacy. Both action and speech need to be in constant contact with others. If these occur in private, no one will hear or see them and they will, for all purposes, not exist. Action corresponds, in Arendt's philosophy, to birth. Action and speech reveal a uniqueness of man. "Action and speech are so closely related because the primordial and specifically human act must at the same time contain the answer to the question asked of every newcomer: 'Who are you?' The disclosure of who somebody is, is implicit in both his words and his deeds . . . many, and even most acts, are performed in the manner of speech" (*Human* 178). It is because of this that it is important for action and speech to be brought forth and exposed to the public.

Labor and action became important during this time because of the introduction of the assembly line and mass production. Labor brings to bear those items that are not permanent, but are used up or discarded, and mass production created more products than a generation could use up. Through the use of machines to create more products, craftsmanship, to some extent, became reduced to labor.

The Industrial Revolution, as its name implies, brought about the invention of machinery to make each person's life easier. Arendt saw these machines as being nothing but substitutes for labor which allowed her to demonstrate how machines may, at some point in the future, replace the need for man in order to create products.

For remembering, passing on, and learning from the modern era, poets, storytellers, and historiographers took the time to write down events and stories to pass on to future generations. The different genres available allowed for the story to reach a larger audience based on each individual's personal taste regarding storytelling. The need to record acts and thoughts became very apparent during this time as recording was made easier through the telegraph and phonograph. Gutenberg had introduced the printing press years before, but recording the voice made it easier to share stories with others. And, because it is difficult for one to tell his or her own story, "it is not the actor but the storyteller who perceives and 'makes' the story" (Arendt, *Human* 192). Without the men and women who wrote down the events and actions of others, we would have little record of what happened in the past with which to gauge our own actions and responses.

Moving into the mid- to late twentieth century, and the early twenty-first century, the understanding of public has again shifted. However, in Arendt's understanding of the modern public, politics is no longer conducted publicly. Two areas in which Arendt's public has not changed from the modern understanding: public is not political and public is where men and women still meet to discuss things that affect the community. One thing that has shifted is the understanding of community. With the advent of technological communication abilities, the community is now the entire world as any person, no matter where he or she is located, can discuss anything with any other person, as long as they are somehow connected technologically.

Today, the public realm is first and foremost permanent. It is difficult, if not impossible, to have a public space, where individuals congregate, that is not always present. It was imperative for Arendt that the public could not be limited to the present time. For her, the public must plan on the past and the future in its creation and its continuity. If an area or idea exists only for the lifetime of an individual, it falls more into the realm of the private than the public. The public is common, that which, according to Arendt, "transcends our life-span into past and future alike . . . It is what we have in common not only with those who live with us, but also with those who were here before and those who will come after us" (*Human* 55). The need for anything that is permanent to be public does not necessarily require that anything that is public needs to be permanent. It is just the visibility of the space, item or idea that is required in order for any type of permanence to exist.

This permanence also requires that others have experienced or felt it, that the public is tangible. The product may be a story or a feeling, but more individuals than just the actor must have experienced it. It may be the storyteller reliving the adventure told through the words of the actor, but the experience must become tangible for it to be public.

The fact that the public is tangible makes it the perfect location for any act of greatness to be recognized and noticed. Arendt explains that "no activity can become excellent if the world does not provide a proper space for its exercise. Neither education nor ingenuity nor talent can replace the constituent elements of the public realm, which make it the proper place for human excellence" (*Human* 49). Because, as was discovered in previous generations, in order for something to be excellent, it must be seen by others, and even though the understanding of the public realm has shifted, this is still the case today. This recognition comes through the common area of the public and through the ability for others to hear about such greatness. The Olympic games, started in Ancient Greece and continuing today, demonstrate the need for public recognition for greatness, as do all sporting events. Although greatness can include many different areas, sporting events are a universal example of the need for public recognition. This need for greatness requires a public realm in which to act.

An area of change is the emergence of the necessities of life—food, clothing, and shelter—in the public realm. By bringing the household activities into the public realm, the private realm has been limited to that of intimate activities. However, certain areas of the private realm have benefited in public. The African proverb, "It takes a village to raise a child" is a perfect example of the household benefiting by being brought into the public realm.

This proverb expands on the notion that it takes more than two people, the parents, to raise a child—teachers, family members, and others must also be involved in the child's life.

The village or, more specifically, the people of the village can benefit each other because they live in proximity to each other. Arendt notes that this proximity creates a "web of human affairs" which allows a connection of relationships to develop because people live together in the public realm (*Human* 183–184). This web creates connections and experiences which join people together in ways which reach far beyond the political understanding of the public through previous generations.

These human relationships also help create a reality. Without human connections and exchanges, there are many events that are not thoroughly experienced. Arendt explains that in order for something to appear "real" it must be seen and/or experienced by others. This need to share all emotions and experiences with others envelops the household into the public. Take one of the most private emotions—love—for example. When two people fall in love, they do not share that emotion only between the two of them; they tell their friends and family and, usually, hold a large public event when they decide to marry. This very public display brings a very private, even intimate, moment into the public realm in order for it to become real and recognized by the community.

The public realm can also be associated with the term "world." This term means those things that people have in common. By bringing people together based on commonality, the world creates an area for communication to occur and ideas to be shared, but not a world that allows us to step on or fall over each other—literally and ideologically (Arendt, *Human* 52). The public allows people to share ideas but also creates a space of individuality to distinguish one person from another, allowing new and unique ideas and creations to flourish.

One drawback to existing purely in a public realm is that a life may become shallow. "While it retains its visibility, it loses the quality of rising into sight from some darker ground which must remain hidden if it is not to lose its depths in a very real, non-subjective sense" (Arendt, *Human* 71). Because a life lived in public has no hidden or private sector, it is difficult for anyone living a purely public life to have any mystery or discretion to it. This type of life can become only about appearance with no depth to the character of the individual. One example of public life becoming shallow relates to individual description. Arendt explains that the "moment we want to say *who* somebody is, our very vocabulary leads us astray into saying *what* he is; . . . we begin to describe a type or a 'character' . . . with the result that his specific uniqueness escapes us" (*Human* 181). Next time you go to introduce two people, try not introducing them by their profession or hobbies; describe their personality . . . you will find it quite difficult as we are a community of labels and description.

The current era is not immune to the benefits of storytelling. Arendt explains that every life can be told as a story and that history is just the human story which has no beginning and no end. At best, Arendt believes that we might be able to isolate the original actor of the story, but even he does not know the final outcome of his actions (*Human* 184–185). Once again, for all intents and purposes, the storyteller and the actor remain separate individuals. Although there may be some stories that are told by the actor, many historical and biographical events are told from an outsider's point of view, allowing for a more intersubjective view of the situation.

Examining the public realm throughout history provides a solid ground to understanding how the area of life that is shared by most, if not all of humanity, has evolved into its current state and the current understanding that humanity holds of this shared space in the world. After all, "that civilizations can rise and fall, that mighty empires and great cultures can decline and pass away without external catastrophes . . . is due to this peculiarity of the public realm, which, because it ultimately resides on action and speech, never altogether loses its potential character" (Arendt, *Human* 199–200). The public realm exists today, existed in the past, and more than likely, will exist long into the future. It also provides a solid ground on which to begin our exploration into the realm of the social.

SOCIAL

The social, for Arendt, is a modern phenomenon which has multiple nuances in her work. Benhabib writes:

> There are three dominant meanings of the term *social* in Arendt's work. At one level, the *social* refers to the growth of a capitalist commodity exchange economy. At the second level, it refers to aspects of mass society. In the third and least investigated sense, the *social* refers to sociability, to the quality of life in civil society and civic associations. (23)

The works which are associated most closely with the social include *Rahel Varnhagen*, *The Origins of Totalitarianism*, and *The Human Condition*. Although the above quote mentions three meanings of the social, it is more an evolution of the concept than separate meanings. This evolution occurred through Arendt's life experiences and the time in which she wrote each work. Her major concern with the social was the tendency of people to begin thinking like the majority—groupthink—and losing the ability to have and/or to express a unique thought. This concern never leaves Arendt, but the topics regarding the nature of the collective thought evolve throughout her work.

Although these works were published within seven years of each other (between 1951 and 1958), their writing spanned almost twenty years, allowing life experiences and scholarly research to affect Arendt's understanding of this term. Arendt began work on *Rahel Varnhagen* while she was in Paris between 1933 and 1939; she began *The Origins of Totalitarianism* in 1947; and she began *The Human Condition* in 1952. During this time, Arendt lived in several different countries and experienced different forms of government and different cultures. Arendt's largest concern with the social is that it will become an all-encompassing realm. The loss of the public and private realms concerns Arendt because these are the basis of the human community for her. The absorption of these realms into the social is apocalyptic for Arendt.

Another concern regarding the social for Arendt is that many people want to get involved in all activities and work. In the social realm people are not happy with just observing; they want to do. And, for Arendt, if you are not skilled in the task, the "doing" undermines the craft and the excellence of the product (Arendt, *Human* 161). This problem with unskilled involvement in the work is best described in the idiom "too many cooks in the kitchen." The craftsman needs to work in seclusion in order to create his product. Inexperienced people who want to get involved remove the skill and talent needed to create the artifact with the excellence of the craftsman.

One understanding of the social to be examined is that of a "capitalist commodity exchange economy." Growing a country for no reason, other than financial power, was unthinkable for Arendt. Her interpretation allows a glimpse into her personal experience with the Nazis taking control and attempting to grow the regime by conquering other governments without any thought as to why a specific area should be included except for a grab for power. This was especially apparent to Arendt when it came to democratic governments and the capitalist mentality of gaining capital solely for the purpose of gaining capital. Her concern was founded in the idea that overtaking others just for the thrill of doing so when "a World War was needed to get rid of Hitler, which was shameful precisely because it was also comic" (*Origins* 132). This type government and growth provided a shared mentality for the necessity to grow for economic purposes no matter the cost or detriment to the country or its citizens. This is the concern that Arendt experienced with the economic aspect of the social realm.

The scientific thought that corresponds to this development is no longer political science by "national economy" or "social economy" or *Volkswirtschaft*, all of which indicate a kind of "collective housekeeping"; the collective of families economically organized into the facsimile of one superhuman family is what we call "society," and its political form of organization is called "nation." We therefore find it difficult to realize that according to ancient thought on these matters, the very term "political economy" would have been a contradiction in terms: whatever was "economic," related to the life of the individual and the survival of the species, was a non-political, household affair by definition (Arendt, *Human* 28–29). Economic factors, which used to be in the realm of the private, have become a community concern, moving them into the realm of the social. Arendt continues "politics is nothing but a function of society, that action, speech, and thought are primarily superstructures upon social interest, is not a discovery of Karl Marx but on the contrary is among the axiomatic assumptions that Marx accepted uncritically from the political economists of the modern age" (*Human* 33). A major concern for Arendt was "a complete victory of society" with a political agenda that is "ruled by an 'invisible hand,' namely, by nobody" (*Human* 44–45). This concern of rule by nobody can be seen in many mass cultures where no one can verify who makes the rules, just that the rules must be followed. Through mass society and economic factors, man, as an individual, has been somewhat consumed by the need to coordinate behavior and consolidate economic concerns together in order for him to live with others.

An example of this economic consolidation can be seen in Pittsburgh, Pennsylvania, where a "500-unit middle-class townhouse community called Pennsbury Village became, in 1977, the only private condominium complex in the United States ever to form its own municipality" (Stark 10). Once the separation was complete, "Borough manager Irv Foreman recalls, 'We sat down, the condo association and the municipality, to divvy up powers, and for tax reasons we gave everything we might otherwise have purchased privately, . . . to the public government'" (Stark 10). This example shows both capitalist economy and mass society mentality at work. How can this work best for the community, but be the most cost-effective for community members? It is this type of question that has been raised by the emergence of society.

Another area of conformism that relates to the economic understanding of the social realm is that of labor emerging from the private realm. Labor being introduced into the social realm provided the need for individuals to hold property independently from others, which allowed for the growth of organizations outside of the government to manage and protect these holdings.

This growth outside of the government brought about the beginning of mass society. This mass society involved large groups of people getting together to create products, protect private property, and introduce norms and mores that were expected from its members.

Through his interpretation of Arendt's work, Baehr provides a clearer understanding of the social than Arendt provides in *The Human Condition*. This is furthered through *The Attack of the Blob: Hannah Arendt's Concept of the Social*. This text interprets Arendt's understanding of the social as a "living, autonomous agent determined to dominate human beings, absorb them, and render them helpless" (Pitkin 3). As this definition demonstrates,

Arendt does not feel that the social is a productive move for humans. Her feeling is that the social caused humans to lose their freedoms. Pitkin's understanding of Arendt's social as "an evil monster from outer space" that is "destroying us, gobbling up our distinct individuality and turning us into robots that mechanically serve its purposes" (4) lends itself to the title of Pitkin's text, based on a science-fiction movie of the 1950s. Pitkin then becomes a bit more focused on the true intention of Arendt's concept of the social: "The real-world problem that Arendt intended her concept of the social to address . . . concerns the gap between our enormous, still-increasing powers and our apparent helplessness to avert the various disasters—national, regional, and global—looming on our horizon" (6). This quote can be understood to mean technology; not just computer technology, but also things which previously seemed impossible to accomplish, such as the atomic bomb or the moon landing.

Ramsey specifies the understanding of a technological world, through a reading of Heidegger in which the only "dangers are that we see only calculation and objective truths as the necessary components of orienting ourselves in the world" (463–464). This provides a greater understanding of Heidegger's concern with technology, and also provides a greater, philosophical definition of technology that expands its understanding to be more than just computer technology. The social deals with technology, more specifically, Arendt's concern with our ability to deal with the consequences that technology, such as nuclear weapons, could trigger. Her understanding of the social in terms of technology had to do with how these advancements would impact the world as a whole because the results would impact more than just a single community or public.

Another concern with technology had to do with machines gaining control of one of the most human activities, laboring. For laborers, Arendt writes, "the world of machines has become a substitute for the real world, even though this pseudo world cannot fulfil the most important task of the human artifice, which is to offer mortals a dwelling place more permanent and more stable than themselves" (*Human* 152). The fact that machines could have such a large influence in society was a concern for Arendt because there was little knowledge of how the machines would change labor and how the machines would impact man and the interactions between men and the world.

Arendt also had concerns with the social in terms of the loss of the household and family unit and the rise of groupthink based on social opinion. "The striking coincidence of the rise of society with the decline of the family indicates clearly that what actually took place was the absorption of the family unit into corresponding social groups" in which "one common interest and one unanimous opinion is tremendously enforced by sheer number, actual rule exerted by one man, representing the common interest and the right opinion, could eventually be dispensed with" (*Human* 39–40). This unanimous opinion was of great concern for Arendt in terms of the loss of unique thought and individual opinion. This is the largest understanding of group-think and also the biggest concern for Arendt. By agreeing with the majority just because it is the majority, Arendt fears that humanity will not always be advancing in the correct and best direction.

This groupthink can be driven by social status, allowing those with the highest status to control social opinion. Although mass society supposedly equalizes all, there remains a hierarchical structure in even the most democratic of societies. This hierarchy can be based on financial or political power, but the hierarchy exists no matter how much "equality for all" is expressed.

Arendt's concern with the social, specifically mass society, is that a form of despotism may occur. She states that "the unfortunate truth about behaviorism and the validity of its 'laws' is that the more people there are, the more likely they are to behave and the less likely to tolerate non-behavior" (*Human* 43). Arendt's experience with many members of her intellectual cohort joining the Nazi party, because it was either join or be silenced, provided her with the foundation for great concern regarding this type of behavior. This situation occurred in Arendt's life and provided a lifelong aversion to any form of society in which one opinion or idea held the majority of individuals captive through alienation without compliance to the ideas of the majority.

This conformism can be seen today in the cliques formed by teenagers and in the gang subculture. This reality can also be seen in the media through the movie *The Stepford Wives*. This constitutes a concern because it can lead to the loss of the individual and the creativity that comes from thinking "outside of the box." Belonging to a specific social class, for Arendt, has replaced belonging to a family. The social class affords the protection and comfort that the household once provided. This is a concern because the social class lacks the historical and situational ground that the family provided through generations of traditions and stories of shared ancestors and experiences.

Taking the idea of social class in another direction, the third nuance of the social, for Arendt, is that of sociability. This sociability can be best demonstrated through the salons in Europe pre- and post-World War II. Benhabib explains the salons as "a curious space that is in the home yet public, that is dominated by women yet visited and frequented by men, that is highly mannered yet egalitarian, and that is hierarchical toward 'outsiders' and egalitarian toward its members" (22). For Arendt, the social is more than economic growth and mass society; it also deals with interactions with those who would seem unlikely. Arendt's focus on this area is expected because "as a historian of anti-Semitism and totalitarianism, she focuses on transformations occurring in these spheres of modern societies as they eventually lead to the formation of a mass society" (Benhabib 29–30). By expanding the social beyond the political and economic, Arendt bridges her philosophy into the realm of communication.

The social, as being sociability or society, is best illustrated in *Rahel Varnhagen*. In this work, the groupthink is compartmentalized in the salons of Europe, which were smaller-scale communities that recognized the problem of class structure and discrimination in the larger arena, but did not recognize that the salons had become mini-societies. Although the salons still possessed some form of groupthink it was a small community based on common ideas and attitudes and less on birth right, class structure, politics, or economics. In the salons, people would come together in someone's home to discuss many different things. These individuals would not normally interact in a public situation, but would interact in the salons. The salons allowed individuals to meet and converse on different topics without concern for class or status.

Rahel's salons were one of the most popular to attend. Many different classes of people, with many levels of education and political knowledge, attended her salons. The salons allowed for introspection and also provided a safe place to share ideas and create new and different ways of self-presentation (Benhabib 16). The salons allowed for the individual to become an individual; to break the mold of groupthink and express thoughts that might otherwise be suppressed by the masses.

Rahel experienced much alienation in her life. She was never part of an accepted social group and had become a master at "the art of representing her own life: the point was not to tell the truth, but to display herself; not always to say the same thing to everyone but to each what was appropriate for him" (Arendt, *Rahel* 117). Sharing only bits and pieces of herself allowed Rahel to have "a specific social quality, and of being not only a single person but a person naturally intertwined with many others in the intricacies of social life; of existing simultaneously as mother and as child, as sister and as sweetheart, as citizen and as friend—this she had to learn" *(Rahel* 118). This skill allowed Rahel to become part of society, yet maintain her own personality by sharing those parts of her that were appropriate for any given audience at any given time.

As time moved forward and the community moved into a more civil society, "the forms of sociability and intimacy prefigured by the salons become in part social reality" (Benhabib 17). As the dictatorships faded and people became more independent thinkers, feeling less oppressed, people began communicating *with* each other and not *to* each other. Communication and conversation have become important to society as a result of the salons and a freer government in which the fear of consequences has been removed.

Communication is important as society and community grows and moves forward.

As Arendt's understanding of the social evolved, her fear of the "blob" diminished. Remaining as one part of her concern was the concept of group-think while allowing the aspect of sociability to emerge. The evolution of this term in Arendt's work spans three distinct, yet interrelated, interpretations of the social realm. The economic interpretation, the mass society interpreta-tion, and the sociability interpretation demonstrate how a concept can shift meaning based on a situation or viewpoint. The economic and mass society understandings are best demonstrated through *The Human Condition*, and are the best-known interpretations of Arendt's work with the social. Her earlier works, especially *Rahel Varnhagen*, demonstrate an understanding of the sociability aspect of the social realm as interaction and communication among people for many different reasons. This concept of the social is not the evil blob that Arendt fears—although the concept of group think is still present—but refers to individuals working together, sharing ideas with each other, and having conversations regarding many topics. With the other as-pects of the social still in place, this project will utilize the sociability aspect as it moves forward.

In order to move forward, I must take a step back and address the diary, journal, and blog in terms of Arendt's philosophy regarding public, private, and social. The diary is written to be shared with no one while the author is alive; therefore, the diary undeniably falls into the realm of the private. The journal is written with the knowledge that a limited number of "known" readers would see the journal. This puts the journal in the realm of the public. The public involves a community of individuals with whom the author can interact on a regular basis, such as family and close friends in terms of readers of the journal. Finally, the blog is written with the knowledge of an audience of both known and unknown readers. The personal blog, because of a common interest which unites the blogger and his or her readers, also shall be placed in the public realm. Individuals are asked to participate and engage in conversation about the blog's topics. This conversation creates the connec-tion between reader and blogger, which concretely places the personal blog in the realm of the public.

Chapter Three

Interpersonal Communication and the Role of Communication Technology

Hannah Arendt believed in the necessity of a public realm in order for humans to be productive and to survive. This public realm included the need to communicate with each other. She examined previous philosophers' thoughts on the need to live together and discovered that the understanding of communicating, working, and living together changed dramatically over time. She began her understanding with Plato's allegory of the cave (*The Republic,* Book VII*)* and the need for people to go into the light, where there were other people, in order to share ideas with others. Then she examined Marx's understanding that philosophy and its truth are located in the affairs of men and their common world and can only be understood by living together in society (*The Eighteenth Brumaire of Louis Bonaparte*).

Throughout history the question has been whether interpersonal communication, on a "common" level, is good or bad, or, more specifically, productive or harmful to both the individual and the community as a whole. Arendt identified two well-known scholars' opinions on the subject and summarized her thoughts in *Rahel Varnhagen*: "If we feel at home in this world, we can see our lives as the development of the 'product of nature,' as the unfolding and realization of what we already were. The world in that case becomes a school in the broadest sense, and other people are cast in the roles of either educators or misleaders" (Arendt, *Rahel* 4). By using the example of a school, Arendt acknowledges that there are both good and bad influences which can occur through humans living together. The natural, merely social companionship of the human species was considered to be a limitation imposed upon us by the needs of biological life, which are the same for the human animal as for other forms of animal life. Although the Ancients may have felt that living together was a limitation of biological life, Arendt explains that the benefits of learning through tradition while working and communicating with others outweighs any limitations that might occur. Living together breeds innovation and collaboration. This innovation has led to new ways of communicating with others, who may not be physically close, for intellectual and personal relationships.

The public community is not the location, but the people. Arendt explains that the *polis* is "the organization of the people as it arises out of acting and speaking together" (*Human* 198). In this way, she may consider the idea of an online community, made through blogging or other means, to be a public community—it is the people, not the place; therefore, it should not matter if people are in close physical proximity to one another. Arendt would likely agree that the physical location would not matter in terms of communication or community; the important part of communication and community is the sharing of ideas, opinions, and experiences.

The distance between people is necessary for the public world. "To live together in the world means essentially that a world of things is between those who have it in common, as a table is located between those who sit around it; the world, like every in-between, relates and separates men at the same time" (Arendt, *Human* 52). The world, then, comes between people when they are communicating and interacting with one another. There is no reason that people need to be physically close in order for a community to be created. Distance may be seen as beneficial to the growth of the human race as different locations lead to different experiences and different solutions to sometimes very similar problems. Having the ability, through communication technology, to discuss similar events or concerns may bring a faster solution to a problem or provide insight into new innovations much more quickly.

EVOLUTION OF COMMUNICATION TECHNOLOGY

Humans have always sought mechanical means of extending and enhancing face-to-face communication to efficiently serve needs for security, socialization, collectivization, and fantasy. The result has been the permanatizing and electrifying of the channels of communication that make possible the reproduction of human communication over time and space. Meyrowitz explains, "The evolution of media has decreased the significance of physical presence in the experience of people and events. One can now be an audience to a social performance without being physically present; one can communicate 'directly' with others without meeting in the same place" (*No Sense of Place* vii). Each new technology not only extended the reach of human communication, it also altered the ways in which humans related to information and to each other.

The effects of media, i.e., communication technology, on interpersonal communication can be observed as far back as Socrates. In *Phaedrus*, Socrates stated "once a thing is committed to writing it circulates equally among those who understand the subject and those who have no business with it; a writing cannot distinguish between suitable and unsuitable readers" (Plato 97). Each new communication technology brings about its own challenges and benefits regarding interpersonal communication. This chapter explores the evolution of communication technology, as well as several theories of interpersonal communication that have been created to address this phenomenon.

An examination of the evolution of communication technology, in terms of interpersonal communication, must begin with the spoken word. Speech is the first form of interpersonal communication and, for a long period, was the only "true" form of interpersonal communication. We define speech as a medium to allow for a true examination of communication from the grunts of cavemen to the beginning of media through the spoken word. Then someone invented the new communication technology of writing and suddenly communication took a new form—one that was more permanent and allowed for the evaluation of ideas. However, just as with any technology, there were those who had concerns. Despite concerns with writing, this communication technology allowed for a greater understanding of each individual and the community as a whole. Arendt spoke about the impact of the written word in 1973. During her remarks to the American Society of Christian Ethics, she discussed the impact the written word might have.

> Each time you write something and you send it out into the world and it becomes public, obviously everybody is free to do with it what he pleases, and this is as it should be. I do not have any quarrel with this. You should not try to hold your hand now on whatever may happen to what you have been thinking for yourself. You should rather try to learn from what other people do with it. (*Human* xx)

As this statement demonstrates, Arendt determined that a person could learn from whatever he or she wrote down, not only through writing it, but also by examining what others are doing with the information. By following the intellectual path of a written idea the writer, and others, have the ability to watch the idea grow and expand into areas that the original author may never have thought about. For Arendt, this was a benefit; for Socrates, this would not have been.

After the written word became an accepted form of interpersonal communication, there was a need to make it easier for everyone to obtain copies of written works. In 1440, Johannes Gutenberg invented the movable type printing press. This invention, although not the first printing press, was the first with movable type that made books more affordable for everyone. This communication technology provided a way for interpersonal communication, in the form of books, to be shared with the masses. However, as with any technology there are tradeoffs. The printing press may have provided a way for writing to be shared with the masses but there was a possibility that memory would be confused with knowledge. The concern with the loss of memory increases with each new technology that provides information. McLuhan explains:

> Our conventional response to all media, namely that it is how they are used that counts, is the numb stance of the technological idiot. For the "content" of a medium is like the juicy piece of meat carried by the burglar to distract the watchdog of the mind. The effect of the medium is made strong and intense just because it is given another medium as "content" (18).

It is the medium, not the message, which affects how people react to information. From the beginning, with the written word, media has played a role in how individuals understood the message.

The next interpersonal communication technology invented was the telegraph. This invention allowed information to be shared more quickly across distances. The telegraph, like many other "needed" technologies, grew quickly because the invention of the telegraph allowed people to communicate with those who were not located physically close to them.

The telephone created a more personal communication technology. The telephone allowed people to communicate through technology while still hearing the other person's voice, bridging the distance while allowing an aural connection because the intonation of the voice was heard and emotion could be more clearly interpreted. The telephone appreciably broke through walls and distance and provided a way for people to talk to each other without having to travel distances in order to hear each other's voice.

The next evolutions in communication technology brought about one-to-many communication. Radio, television, and movies provide one-way communication of a message or a form of entertainment. The announcer or performer would communicate from a studio or on the screen and many people would have the ability to react to it at the same time. Donald Horton and R. Richard Wohl recognize "one of the striking characteristics of the new mass media—radio, television, and the movies—is that they give the illusion of face to face relationship with the performer." Because the script was written with the audience's reaction in mind, it appeared that there was a true interpersonal relationship with the character represented.

> The spectacular fact about such personae is that they can claim and achieve an intimacy with what are literally crowds of strangers, and this intimacy, even if it is an imitation and a shadow of what is ordinarily meant by that word, is

extremely influential with, and satisfying for, the great numbers who willingly receive it and share in it.(Horton and Wohl)

This one-to-many communication, while not traditional interpersonal communication, allows for a para-social relationship.

The most recent form of communication technology is computer-mediated communication (CMC). This involves email, websites, social networking, and blogging. Because the communication is with another person, and not the machine itself, CMC is a form of interpersonal communication. This type of communication can be delayed in that both people do not need to be online at the same time, which allows for the opportunity to think about and possibly research a response. With the ability to "think before you speak" in CMC, the respondent has more time to make an informed and well thought-out response; this differs in some ways from face-to-face communication because sometimes the person speaks before thinking . . . not that there has never been a person who "typed without thinking." CMC provides a way for people to communicate throughout the world, including with people they do not know. This is a major advantage of CMC because it allows for the world to become smaller in terms of the ability to communicate, and yet larger in the knowledge and experiences that each individual can gain without the expense of travel. The ability to communicate through technology affords a wealth of ideas and an enlarged conversation. Walt Disney was right: "it's a small world after all."[1]

This small world, achieved through communication technology, requires a shift in communication styles. However, in terms of mediated interpersonal communication, Meyrowitz explains that electronically mediated communication is closer to face-to-face than written communication because of the ability for the receiver to provide feedback ("The Separation" 146). This can be attributed to the statement-response format allowed by CMC which mitigates Socrates' concern for the lack of response available with the written word. CMC brings back the ability, even though the words are written on the screen, for the give and take of communicator and audience interaction. However, Turkle notes that "when technology engineers intimacy, relationships can be reduced to mere connections. And then, easy connection becomes redefined as intimacy. Put otherwise, cyberintimacies slide into cybersolitudes" (16). Although interpersonal mediated communication may make it easier to communicate with one another, and is closer to face-to-face than written communication, interpersonal mediated communication lacks the nonverbal and paraverbal cues that occur in face-to-face communication.

CMC offers the ability for multiple people to engage in communication without leaving their home or office. This ability for communication with no distance barriers allows for a greater reach of the message and more feedback and input into the conversation, but at what cost? Does interpersonal mediated communication make it too easy to collaborate but not connect to others? According to Chesebro and Bonsall, in 1989, "when humans use computers, a dimension of their social condition is ignored. While a large number of human expressions can be conveyed in binary notations, the binary system itself reflects only one feature of human consciousness" (81). The date of the publication is specifically noted because CMC has progressed a long way from 1989, but there is still the concern that CMC can distance people from each other while seemingly connecting them.

One area of concern raised by communication technology is the loss of the "gatekeeper." This loss can be most easily noted through the radio, telephone, and television, prior to the introduction of the personal computer into the home. This upsets many people because of the availability of information to children without any control from adults. The lack of control that parents have over the information that their children can see and the people that they may meet through technology can cause great concern and real problems.

The ability for communication technology to access location and information raises another concern regarding the private aspects of life. Turkle explains this phenomenon: "Only a decade ago . . . it might have seemed intrusive, if not illegal, that my mobile phone would tell me the location of all of my acquaintances within a ten-mile radius. But these days we are accustomed to all this" (15–16). What is the cost of this advancement in technology?

Another way that communication technology creates an invasion of privacy is the ability to store information about individuals so that businesses can target them more easily. This targeted marketing, although an excellent advancement for businesses and government agencies, is an invasion of privacy for the individual.

Communication technology makes it easy to "look things up" instead of knowing things. This becomes a problem of knowing where to look for the information instead of knowing it. "What the Net seems to be doing is chipping away my capacity for concentration and contemplation. Whether I'm online or not, my mind now expects to take in information the way the Net distributes it: in a swiftly moving stream of particles" (Carr 182–183). The collective lack of memory that the constant access to information encourages creates the possibility for culture and history to be lost if the files containing that information are corrupted or deleted.

CMC, especially social networking sites, allows for anything and everything about a person's life to be shared online. And, according to Arendt, "a life spent entirely in public, in the presence of others, becomes, as we would say, shallow. While it retains its visibility, it loses the quality of rising into sight from some darker ground" (*Human* 71). The lack of depth in an individual's life may begin to "dumb down" humanity, and that was a major concern for Arendt and should be a concern for all as CMC becomes the norm and not the exception.

Communication technology can extend a disembodiment of communication. Although most forms of communication can be seen as contact without touch, with the obvious exception of nonverbal communication, the use of mediated communication extends the metaphor even further as media extends the reach of communication beyond those in proximity to each other. No longer do two people need to be in the same space to communicate; they do not even need to be in the same country. This allows for communication to become a global phenomenon and reach more individuals almost instantaneously with the message it conveys, but also provides for a minimum experience as each person may not be fully engaged. Pitkin explains Arendt's concern with technology: "The real-world problem that Arendt intended her concept of the social to address . . . concerns the gap between our enormous, still-increasing powers and our apparent helplessness to avert the various disasters—national, regional, and global—looming on our horizon" (6). Although global communication allows for greater collaboration to the benefit of most, there are also those individuals who use this global reach for evil—the use of CMC for terrorist attacks, for example.

Good or bad, global communication allows an individual the opportunity to gain a better understanding of different people and cultures which also allows for communication to become the preeminent field for carrying out the command, "Know Thyself." An individual begins to gain a better understanding of who they are and what is important to them by communicating with others about issues that are important to him or her. Peters continues, "the key question for twentieth-century communication theory . . . is how wide and deep our empathy for otherness can reach, how ready we are to see 'the human as precisely what is different'" (230). This question continues into the twenty-first century, and I would argue, will go beyond it. Empathy is a uniquely human emotion. How willing are we to step into another person's situation and truly understand it? Can that situation be embraced and clarified through communication? These questions examine the fact that interpersonal communication need not always be face to face. Sharing a life experience in a letter, on a blog, on the telephone, or through an email, provides much information while certain unspoken communication cues are lacking. Sometimes writing can provide more detail and clearer thinking from the sender of the message; however, the lack of nonverbal cues may cause a misinterpretation of the message.

CMC allows communication to occur among people who are not located physically close but who have similar thoughts or ideals that draws them to each other toward a common goal; this may also be referred to as disembodied communication. Pitkin explains that for Arendt, "human interrelationship" has a "structure: a particular, established 'web of relationships,' pattern

Leabharlanna Poiblí Chathair Bhaile Átha Cliath
Dublin City Public Libraries

of institutional organization and habitual practice. Now, institutional structure, as Arendt would hasten to stress, is not physical structure; institutions
are not buildings" (193). This definition of institutions emphasizes that the
institution exists only in the interaction between its members. Spatial infinity
provides a way for communication to occur with those who may be emotionally close to a person, but not physically close. Turkle explains that "online
connections were first conceived as a substitute for face to face contact, when
the latter was for some reason impractical" (13). Disembodied communication also allows for strangers to "meet" through mediated communication
and become emotionally close, possibly even lending emotional support or a
different type of friendship than an individual could receive from those physically close to him or her.

INTERPERSONAL COMMUNICATION THEORIES

Examining the different theories associated with interpersonal communication and communication technology will help to ground this study and provide a clearer understanding of how communication changed due to the use
of interpersonal technology. The interpersonal communication theories this
chapter will examine include boundary management/communication privacy
management and para-social framework.

Communication privacy management (CPM) established by Sandra Petronio and others examines how people decide which information about themselves and their lives they want to share with others, as well as which others
they share this information with. The goal of CPM "is to offer a theoretical
perspective that suggests a way to understand the tension between revealing
and concealing private information" (Petronio, "Translational," 218). The
tension between revealing and concealing has only become stronger with the
advent of social networking websites, some of which were started with less
than noble intentions.[2] This determining of revealing or concealing creates
guidelines or boundaries for each individual.

CPM is also known as boundary management theory because it uses
boundaries as a way to determine what information should be shared and
what information should be kept private. It provides a way to balance the two
areas. This balancing must fall within the comfort zone of each individual.
What one person considers private information, another person may willingly share with close friends and family, while a third may share this information with anyone who will listen. Why does the definition of private information differ so greatly between individuals? The definition differs to each
person because each individual has a tolerance for what information may be
shared and which should be kept private. Thus, communication boundaries
become a private matter.

CPM theory focuses on communication and the information shared more so than the person sharing. By highlighting the information instead of the person, CPM focuses on what individuals consider private information and less emphasis is placed on the individuals involved in the sharing process. This focus lends itself to allowing the information to take the primary role in an exchange. Instead of the focus being on what people want to know about each other, or what the individual wants people to know about him or her, the focus is on what information the individual is willing to share with others and which information each individual considers private. This also leads into the next question of who should information be shared with? Is the information something that an individual would share with anyone who asked or is the information something that he or she would only share with those people that he or she knows well? Or, is this information that the individual would share with no one else?

CPM examines the nature of the relationship between individuals to determine a connection between the information shared and the strength of the connection with those with whom the information is shared. "The contextualization or how the dialectical tensions are situated for privacy management assumes that whenever private information is disclosed, a privacy boundary is formed around the participants" (Petronio, *Boundaries* 22). The relationship between the individuals may determine which type of information is shared between them and which type of information is withheld. For example, a teenager may tell his or her friends about a date but he or she may not feel comfortable sharing the same information with his or her parents. The relationship that is formed between individuals determines the level of sharing that occurs.

One important aspect of CPM that needs to be addressed is that of what happens to the information once it is shared. How does the individual sharing know that those who know his or her private information will not share that information with someone he or she does not want to know? CPM addresses this through the argument that once someone knows a piece of information, they become a co-owner of it; therefore, they also become responsible for whether or not the information may be shared. There is also some coordination which must take place between the sender of the information and the receivers to determine who the information may be shared with. By telling someone not to tell anyone else, an individual begins to establish the guidelines which the group, or co-owners of the information, are expected to follow in terms of the information shared. Have you ever told someone, or been told, "Do not share this with anyone" or "This information is just between us"? If so, you have co-owned private information.

This new understanding of the importance of focusing on the information helps to remove the therapeutic aspect of focusing on the individual. Petronio states that "claiming that we needed to have private information at the core changed the very way I began to think about the concept. Privacy became the root of understanding instead of (or in addition to) the self" ("Road" 195). This theory then allows us a new way to examine the issue of privacy using the information as the fulcrum creating the shift of focus toward communication and away from the individual. The creators of CPM state that "rather than searching for the meaning of 'self information,' an examination of 'private information' became the focus. This reallocation of privacy gave us more specificity about the kind of information we were seeking to understand" (Petronio, "Road," 195). By focusing on what information individuals consider private, CPM allows for a more targeted examination of communication than focusing on all information that is shared about the self. There is such a concern about privacy because it allows us to feel unique and allows us to feel that we own any and all information about ourself. Especially in the age of the Internet and identity theft, it is important for individuals to believe that they own all information that pertains to them. This sense of ownership of information allows each of us to have control over our lives.

Control over one's information is important for all individuals. Even celebrities try to maintain a sense of privacy and control over some aspects of their lives. A recent celebrity example of this need for control is the quick and private divorce settlement of Katie Holmes and Tom Cruise. The divorce was filed and settled very quickly and no terms of the agreement, to date, have been leaked to the media. The need for privacy appears to have driven the couple to quickly resolve any differences so that their personal matters did not become public news fodder. This demonstrates Petronio's claim that "ownership and control are rudimentary to understanding the way people define and handle their private information" *(Road* 202). Control of information is very important, if not crucial, to some people's sense of self and boundaries with other people. However, if we do not share information, we do not allow anyone to get to know us and possibly build a relationship with us. By setting standards for how information is shared, an individual creates a sense of security surrounding his or her private information.

If privacy is so important, why do people decide to share any information? One reason is intimacy. "Intimacy reflects all of the aspects of a close relationship. Disclosing private information may be one way intimacy is established" (Petronio, *Boundaries* 5). However, there are reasons other than intimacy that people share private information. Some include an outlet to relieve a burden, a way to gain control, and an avenue for self-expression. It is for the last reason, self-expression, that many people begin writing a personal blog.

Exactly how does a person decide what information to disclose to others, either on a one-to-one basis or through mediated communication? There are five primary principles to demonstrate how people deal with disclosure of private information. These five principles include the fact that individuals feel that they own any private information about themselves; that they have the right to control that information; that they decide who to share that information with; that they trust the co-owners of that information to retain the understood privacy; and, finally, that privacy management can become volatile (Petronio "Translational," 219). These principles are the basis of CPM and help to determine how to better understand and manage the privacy of our own information.

One key factor in CPM theory is that disclosure and privacy are not separate entities, they are tied together. This tie between disclosure and privacy relates to the issue which Arendt addressed regarding the blurring of public and private. As the need for this theory became evident, Arendt's philosophical concern was brought to light as reality.

CPM addresses the sharing or oversharing from both the sender's and receiver's point of view. From the sender's perspective, it may become awkward if the information is not received as he or she had hoped; however, from the receiver's perspective, they will never be able to unlearn what they have learned which can be a result of oversharing. The oversharing that has become rampant on the Internet, and especially on social networking sites and personal blogs, creates an abundance of situations in which the receiver feels uncomfortable by what is shared. This may lead to someone no longer visiting a blog or to blocking a person's postings on a social networking site.

Petronio addresses the connection of technology and privacy in her introduction to *Boundaries of Privacy: Dialectics of Disclosure*: "two interwoven features of our lives today and in the future are *technology* and *globalization. . . .* we have already begun to experience the *personal and interpersonal* opportunities and problems of globalization and technology. The opportunities are spectacular and will surely increase geometrically in years to come" (*Boundaries* xiii). The opportunities which Petronio mentions may well include the social networking sites, such as LinkedIn, Facebook, and Twitter, which did not exist at the time of her publication. With Child and Pearson she examined blogging specifically in a 2009 study involving college students that determined the importance of balancing the needs for contact and privacy among college students who blogged. Boundary management theory will be useful as this study moves forward in examining how bloggers decide what information to share on their personal blog.

Another interpersonal communication theory that will be useful is the para-social framework as created by Horton and Wohl in 1956. Horton and Wohl explain that "one of the striking characteristics of the new mass media—radio, television, and the movies—is that they give the illusion of face-to-face relationship with the performer. . . .We propose to call this seeming face-to-face relationship between spectator and performer a para-social relationship." Utilizing this theory in terms of CMC we will also look at the unknown, or virtually known, other in terms of the para-social relationship.

Many people feel that the relationships they have online are equivalent to face-to-face relationships because sometimes the communication may be more frequent in virtual relationships (see Walther 1996). One of the features of this theory, which seamlessly moves into the realm of CMC, is that of intimacy. Replacing the role of the persona of the performer with the blogger demonstrates that personal relationships are possible through CMC. "The spectacular fact about such personae is that they can claim and achieve an intimacy with what are literally crowds of strangers" and the blogger's intimacy may be "extremely influential with, and satisfying for, the great numbers who willingly receive it and share in it" (Horton and Wohl). Many people who communicate with others solely online have been communicating with some people longer than they have known many people in real life. This allows the relationships formed through CMC to be just as strong as those which occur face to face.

The para-social relationship theory can be applied to CMC. The relationships between a performer and the audience provide a social context which allows everyday understandings of social and group interaction to be examined and confirmed. Personal blogging provides an avenue for those who are busy with work or family obligations to have a way of sharing day-to-day activities and interests with others. As life becomes busier, the personal blog allows for sharing and friendships at a time that is convenient for all parties, which may be difficult to do in today's over-scheduled society.

One of the phenomena that Meyrowitz discusses in terms of para-social relationships is that in which the performer does not die. Because the performance has been recorded and, therefore, is still available after the perfomer's death, the audience still has access to that person. Many blogs can be shown as examples of those that live on after they have passed. Two examples are: Eve Markvoort, twenty-five, of 65redroses.livejournal.com who passed away on March 27, 2010 from cystic fibrosis and five-month-old Avery Lynn Canahuati of averycan.blogspot.com who passed away on April 30, 2012 from spinal muscular atrophy. Both of these blogs continue to have active postings from family members and friends trying to keep Eve and Avery alive in the hearts of their blog followers and to help raise awareness and research monies for their respective diseases. These examples substantiate Meyrowitz's claim that the relationship with the deceased blogger is not destroyed, but frozen at the time of their passing as outlined in the para-social relationship. Though no one else will be able to meet Eve or Avery in person, many have begun to read their stories after they passed away and provided emotional or financial support to their families or the foundations established in their names. Eve and Avery live on through CMC.

The final category that needs to be examined is that of mediated interpersonal communication. Mediated interpersonal communication is any communication in which some form of technology is introduced into a face to face interaction. Mediated interpersonal communication does not need to occur in the same location, or even at the same time because technology allows for these elements to be secondary. Any communication between two people that is not directly face to face is therefore a form of interpersonal mediated communication. Creating a general category for any form of communication that is not directly face-to-face allows for a more direct study of any form of media.

The type of interpersonal mediated communication which is especially important to this study is that which involves using the medium of the computer. There are two areas of communication which involve the computer. The first is a person-computer interpersonal encounter. Through this encounter, the person communicates with the machine or, more precisely, with a program running on the machine. The other area of communication which involves the computer is such that the person communicates through the computer to another individual, and not directly with the computer. It is this second form of CMC that this project focuses on. Communicating through the computer advances Marshall McLuhan's famous statement that "the medium is the message." Does using a computer as the medium through which people communicate truly change the message? Or does it just make it more convenient to share the message with others who may or may not be physically close to the sender?

EVOLUTION OF MEDIA

One of the benefits of Horton and Wohl's research involves the understanding of the evolution of media. An evolution, although argued by some, which allows people to communicate globally as if the parties were standing right next to each other. The technology allows for international communication on a personal level creating a global neighborhood.

Another theorist that must be examined in the context of media evolution is Paul Levinson. His view of the evolution of media expands upon the technological advances into the psychological advances of making mediated communication more life-like than mediated. In his work *Human Replay: A Theory of the Evolution of Media*, Levinson explains his idea that communication technology's goal is to make mediated communication as life-like as possible. Humans in a "'pre-technological' state see in colors rather than black-and-white, speak in voices rather than Morse code, usually hear sounds emanating from a variety of sources rather than a single source, the pattern of media change becomes very clear: media are evolving . . . to reproduction of human or 'pretechnological' forms of communication" (Levinson, *Human Replay* 1). This observation of media allows us to see that the evolution of media attempts to bring communication back to its most natural form, while enhancing it through collapsing time and space so that communication is not limited to those with whom we have direct face-to-face contact with at a time when the need or desire to communicate comes upon us, but provides the ability for communication to be non-linear, but still interpersonal through the use of mediated communication. Reeves and Nass also noticed a tie between interpersonal communication and mediated communication explaining that people interact with media in a way that is similar to interactions with other people. They note "Everyone expects media to obey a wide range of social and natural rules. All these rules come from the world of interpersonal interaction, and from studies about how people interact with the real world. But all of them apply equally well to media" (Reeves and Nass 5). The connection between interpersonal communication and mediated communication provides a well-researched area of study on which to stand as the research moves forward into interpersonal mediated communication.

Moving away from television and computer programs and into social media, Levinson, in *New New Media*, explains that one of the key aspects of the new new media is that they are social. They provide a human dynamic that is missing in most other forms of media. This social aspect of the media, according to Levinson, set the new new media apart from new media such as the Internet. The new new media allow each and every user to create content if they choose (Levinson, *New New,* 4). One aspect which Levinson points out, and which is important to this research, is that although all new new media have a social aspect, there are certain new new media that "are primarily social in that their main purpose is to connect people" (*New New* 5–6). These media include blogs, Facebook, Twitter, and other social networking sites.

Blogs are an exemplar of the new new media, according to Levinson. "A blog can be written on a moment's notice, can be amended indefinitely and can last forever. Anyone, including any reader, can become a blogger. Consumers of other new new media daily become producers of new new media in this way. Readers can also contribute to the narrative of the blog by writing comments" *(New New* 12). The term new new media brings about some comparisons to Web 2.0, but the new new media is focused completely on interactions between people and not just a person and a computer which is what makes the new new media so important in the field of communication.

Social media, given its name because of the two-way communication aspect, can bring about a type of classification of individuals. Whether interacting with an individual that is an online friend, i.e., someone that a person has never met in real life, a friend or a family member there is a type of role that is assigned to that individual. These roles can allow the user or blogger to determine what information that particular individual might see. According to Pitkin, Arendt would understand that "in mass society, the social is a leveling force, normalizing all into conventional patterns of behavior, but this is merely an extension of what society has already done and meant: forcing people into arbitrary categories" (Pitkin 183). Consider how you classify people daily; you may have your work friends, your school friends, your neighbors, and your family, for example. For Arendt, this is acceptable because it is necessary. And, while Arendt may not advocate social media in its current state, she did recognize the inherent need to classify people into categories for a better understanding of how to relate to them. Choosing categories by which to classify and define people is a problem for Arendt only if these procedures are used to replace politics but she does understand the need to categorize people in other aspects of life.

Reeves and Nass note that when interacting with media people tend to ignore the media as if it were not there and interact as they normally would. This revelation came through their study which states that our brains have not evolved as quickly as media technology has. These "old brains" know that "anything that *seemed* to be a real person or place *was* real" (Reeves and Nass 12). The interactions and interpersonal communication matter most, no matter if they are face to face or mediated.

The interactions and communication that occur through CMC usually lead to dialogue. This term is used in the most basic understanding—two or more people discussing a specific topic. As people comment on a blog and then more people, or the original poster, respond to that comment, a dialogue evolves which involves anyone reading and commenting on that particular blog post. This medium allows for dialogue to occur between those that are separated by time and space. The lack of spatial limits on dialogue in the blogosphere creates an arena with considerable opportunity for a complete and well-informed conversation to occur. Where a person physically is does not matter as long as the persons in dialogue are emotionally or intellectually connected. One constant about dialogue is that dialogue cannot lead to one particular outcome because every contributor to the dialogue owns a part of it and cannot control what the others may or may not contribute. This allows the dialogue to belong to no one individually, but every participant collectively.

DIALOGUE

The give-and-take of a conversation between individuals is known as dialogue. Dialogue must be based in reality and grounded in the present; therefore, interactions in MUDs (multi-user games) are not technically dialogue because they are not based in reality. However, since most personal blogs are based in reality and are happening in real time to the blogger, any interactions between a blogger and his or her commenters can be considered dialogue.

Through dialogue, an individual not only learns about the other people in the conversation, but also learns more about him- or herself. Dialogue, then, can be seen as a way to self-understanding, as well as a way to understand others. Both the other and the individual's reaction to the other are needed in order to invite self-understanding in this context.

Dialogue allows for opinions, arguments, and revelations to guide an individual to a better understanding of his or her stance on many subjects. And without the interaction with others, through dialogue, the individual only thinks that he or she understands his or her true feelings on a subject. Bahktin explains that dialogue is needed as a way for humans to become "able or competent to perceive in ourselves the given whole of our own personality" (5). Dialogue, whether face-to-face or mediated, allows one to gain perspective on his or her stance on any given topic or situation.

Dialogue allows for an individual to "know thyself." Mediated communication allows an individual to have a larger group to engage in dialogue with than typical face-to-face communication would allow. Therefore, mediated communication provides for a greater sounding board to help an individual know him- or herself on many levels and on many different subjects. However, the greater ability to know oneself on many levels can lead to a overzealous focus on oneself, most commonly referred to as narcissism.

NARCISSISM

One of the drawbacks to mediated communication, especially mediated communication that is created by an individual based solely on personal opinion and not on facts, is narcissism. By providing an outlet for anyone's voice to have a say, CMC provides an entrance into a therapeutic culture and individual mindset of "it's all about me." Christopher Lasch explains that living "for the moment is the prevailing passion. . . . We are fast losing the sense of historical continuity, the sense of belonging to a succession of generations originating in the past and stretching into the future" (5). This concern with self over history or future is one of the reasons that many people no longer have a connection with their family or with their personal history. Also, the concern with self makes it difficult to be concerned with future generations. When did this shift begin? "The fight for the greater good of the 1960s became looking out for number one by the 1980s. Parenting became more indulgent, celebrity worship grew, and reality TV became a showcase of narcissistic people" (Twenge and Campbell 4). Once the "Me" generation began, the focus on the world and consequences of the individual's actions for others began to diminish.

As the focus on celebrity lifestyles and the desire to learn more about the personal lives of public figures grew, there began a drive to share more of our lives with other people as well. This cultural shift created a shift toward narcissism. However, it is somewhat ironic that without other people to notice how magnificent a narcissist is, there is no way to establish his or her greatness and validate that opinion. Not that the narcissist cares about the other people, except for what those individuals can provide for him or her (Twenge and Campbell 4). This lack of concern for other people demonstrates the difference between those people who have high self-esteem and narcissists.

The American culture of admiring those who are famous and desiring to be like them has fostered the increase of narcissism in our culture. After all, there is a desire to be noticed and recognized, as well as a desire to be famous that comes from a celebrity-worship type of culture. Individuals attempt to create a personal brand. This personal brand may stem from the desire to be more like a celebrity whom one finds intriguing. Public relations and advertising have demonstrated that the right package and the right message can "sell" just about anything to the right individuals, so why not package an individual to "sell" his or her personality and appearance? This attitude has been driven, not only by advertising, but also by the media-focused culture of today. The revelation that narcissism may be a cultural phenomenon has led to the creation of the term "cultural narcissism," defined by Twenge and Campbell as "changes in behavior and attitudes that reflect narcissistic cultural values, whether the individuals themselves are narcissistic or simply caught up in a societal trend" (5). This dialectic of which came first may lead to another important dialectic for this project: which came first, the desire to share private information with others or the communication technology which allows us to do so?

This question begins to be answered by a survey which Twenge and Campbell reference in their book. "In a June 2009 national poll of more than 1,000 college students (57%) also said that one of the main reasons for their generation's self-centeredness was social networking sites such as Facebook, MySpace, and Twitter" (34). As the agreement with the survey statement asserts, the current generation believes that they share more information because the technology exists to do so. However, the question still remains as to why communication technology was originally created. If the current generation of twenty-somethings believes that they are more self-centered because the technology allows them to be, then what was the original motivation for creating social networking sites and their predecessors, personal publishing venues? This question needs to be examined in further research.

These theories and communication aspects which impact disclosure and oversharing in CMC discussed in this chapter are important for the next chapter, which focuses on communication technology, in general, and personal blogging specifically. CMC opened up new ways to communicate and allows for individuals to share information, sometimes without forethought of the consequences. However, communication technology is not all bad; it allows for further input from others around the globe and provides more opportunities for an individual to "Know Thyself."

NOTES

1. For more information on the origin of the song and ride at Disney parks visit: http://disneyland.disney.go.com/disneyland/its-a-small-world/.

2. For an example of the founding of a social network, for less than noble intentions, read *The Accidental Billionaires* by Ben Mezrich regarding the founding of Facebook.

Chapter Four

Personal Blogs: History, Usage, Future—Are We Just Looking for Our 15 Minutes of Fame?

As discussed in chapter 1, blogs started as a way for technology insiders to keep track of and share links of interest with each other. The Internet began to grow so rapidly during its early stages that those involved at the beginning had difficulty keeping up with new webpages. Emails were too time-consuming to send and too numerous to read. Personal homepages began to tell others about the author and soon became a good spot to share the links. This link list began being updated with the latest entry at the top . . . and so began blogging. The list of links became known as a weblog. One typical aspect of the weblog is that all entries were in reverse chronological order. These entries also began to include information about the link or the writer. These webpages became more universal and user-friendly when Pyra, an Internet company, created software to help handle project management. This software "was a website that would take text that a user entered into a form, and post it onto a webpage, with the most recent additions at the top of the page" and Pyra "ended up working more on the in-house tool than on their nominal product. They named their product Blogger and launched it to the world" (Shirky 182). Other companies quickly followed with different versions of software and the blogging revolution began. Blogging was now available to anyone who had access to the Internet and had something to say. And lots of people had lots to say about many different subjects. There was finally a place for them to talk to others with similar interests outside of their normal social circles.

This place became a twenty-first-century public realm. People were able to share ideas with others who had similar interests. Arendt described the public realm as "the world itself, in so far as it is common to all of us and distinguished from our privately owned place in it" (*Human* 52). This description fits perfectly into the blogosphere because the blogosphere allows people to take a step back from mass society and provides a place to gather. The blogosphere brings back the power to gather people together, if only virtually, and get them talking and relating to each other.

Blogs are at the same time public and private. These websites share private information in a public forum and allow others, including complete strangers, to comment on various posts. Blogs are updated regularly, if not daily, and are based on a common theme or topic. Sometimes that theme is "what is happening in my life" other times it is a favorite hobby or an idea. This chapter examines many aspects of personal blogging and finishes with a look into what the future may hold for personal blogs, specifically, and the blogosphere as a whole.

PRIVATE BECOMES PUBLIC

A paraphrase of Andy Warhol's "fifteen minutes of fame" statement that has been attributed to David Weinberger, among others[1] states that "on the Internet, everyone will be famous for fifteen people." This statement is especially true for personal bloggers. Even if the blogger insists that he or she writes only for clarity, most blogs have an audience, either commenters or lurkers (people who only read and do not comment), and the blogger is aware of their presence. It is the ability of others, whether strangers or family members, to read a personal blog that makes it a public medium, even though the subject matter is usually very personal.

The conflict that arises with blogs is that the subject is usually very personal—sometimes intimate, while the medium is public to a fault. Anyone, at least anyone with access to the Internet, can read what is posted on a personal blog. Although many people in younger generations have moved on to social networking sites instead of personal blogs, those in their thirties and above are still writing blogs. Although these blogs may take on a specific focus, i.e., mom blogs, knitting blogs, political blogs, etc., they are still written about the individual, and his or her personal life and opinions will show through in the tone and, sometimes, the topic of a post. Although the blog may specifically be about knitting, a story about something the blogger's child did or something that the blogger saw at work will most likely be written if the blogger finds it "blog-worthy."

Guidelines established by the blogger establish a basis of his or her own view of public (what can be posted on the blog) and private (what is off limits and will not be shared). In her research, Emily Nussbaum interviewed teen bloggers about their experiences with blogging. She recounts one blogger's understanding of blurring private and sharing on his blog: "J.'s sense of private and public was filled with these kinds of contradictions: he wanted his posts to be read, and feared that people would read them, and hoped that people would read them, and didn't care if people read them. . . . He also had his own stringent notions of etiquette" (Kline and Burnstein 353). This type of indecision about what to post is not uncommon in the blogosphere. Each individual blogger establishes what will and will not be shared about his or her life on the blog. "Of course I knew there were limits to what I could say. . . . Legal limits, limits set by embarrassment, by fear or by an old-fashioned sense of decency. How exactly these lines should be defined, however, I did not know. . . . but in my blog I was my own editor" (Ringmar 3). Ringmar's statement helps to begin to clarify that limits are set by more than just the blogger, that there are legal ramifications, as well as personal or professional ramifications to what is posted on a personal blog. Arendt's concern about the blurring of public and private has become reality as some bloggers share too much and some, those without a lot of readers, do not share enough to hold the attention of an audience. Establishing a guideline, whether personal or shared, determining what should and will be shared with others becomes an important aspect for a blogger, and knowing something about Arendt's philosophy may help make that determination simpler.

A benefit to the publicness of a personal blog is the ability to build relationships or a community outside of one's normal social circle. This sense of community can be the result of shared interests, or just everyday happenings that could occur to anyone. A sense of community is formed because "weblogs include software enabling readers' responses to be automatically posted and to appear next to the entry. Thus a dialogical space is created within what is supposed to be an intensely personal space" (Serfaty 53). This dialogic space can go one step further as those that comment can see others' comments and may respond not only to the original post but also to the other comments. The comment section may become a dialogue in and of itself yet still tied to the original blog post. This dialogue, although lacking nonverbal cues, allows for the readers to begin to know each other as they continue to read and comment on each others' blogs.

Another way in which community is formed is because the stories that bloggers share are real and relatable. Talking about something funny that happened on the way to the office or a story about something that your spouse or child did can be highly relatable to a large audience. These are the types of stories that appear on personal blogs on a regular basis.

Bloggers also form a community through blogrolls. Blogrolls are links either on the sidebar of the first page of the blog, or on a separate page. Bloggers add links to those sites which draw them in; it is not important if they know the other blogger or not. Something about the blogger or the topic the blogger frequently writes about has drawn the attention of the person who linked to his or her blog, and a link on his or her blogroll makes it easier to return to read more at a later time. The blogroll helps in creating a community. Who a blogger reads helps to define who the blogger is in terms of the blogosphere, just like the people a person connects with in real life helps to define who he or she becomes. After all, Stone writes, "if a blog is the online version of you, then the blogosphere is the online version of our world, our home" (111). Understanding this fact may help bloggers better determine which information they want to share and who they want to link to; after all, social groups, even virtual ones, help to determine how others see you.

The links on a personal blog also help to extend the public aspect of the blog. Links provide connections in the blogosphere. These connections can link to other people that the blogger follows or other links that the blogger finds interesting. Also, if the blogger has another website, the list of links may include his or her other projects. The links "mimic the social clustering that happens naturally all over the planet" (Stone 194). Take a look around: people gather in groups that share similar interests every day, so why should the gathering on the Internet be any different? Blogs allow for a larger reach of people with similar interests, but the readers and bloggers still have some type of connection or there would be no reason for the reader to keep visiting and certainly no reason for the blogger to link back to the reader's blog—not that all blog readers necessarily have a blog.

Links are important in the blogosphere. Stone calls them "the currency of the blogosphere" (91). The more people who link to a blog, the more likely others who read the first blog will follow the link and find something of interest at the new blog as well. After all, links do not happen haphazardly. If a blogger realizes that another blog has linked to his or her site, it is likely that the first will reciprocate and provide a link to the second site. Links are often used by bloggers to keep track of sites of interest and allow for the blogger to return to the site without trying to remember all of the different addresses, similar to "favorites" in a web browser. Remember, blogging started as a list of links, and that portion still exists today. This linking and sharing of links adds credibility and traffic to a blog. If people visit a blog that has added a link to a new blog, those people may click on the link to see if there is something of interest on the new site as well. Thus, the more people that link to a blog, the more likely that other people will follow and continue visiting if there is something of interest on the new site. Brad Graham explains this quid pro quo: "My weblog is linked from several others, and theirs from mine. We are a community, of sorts, a small town sharing gossip and news, recreation and sport, laughter and tears, all for the commonweal. And, for the most part, we're friendly to strangers" (Perseus Publishing Editors 39). This phrase, "friendly to strangers," leads to the need for a clearer understanding of friendship. C. S. Lewis helps with this understanding: "Friendship, I have said, is born at the moment when one man says to another 'What! You too? I thought that no one but myself . . .' But the common taste or vision or point of view which is thus discovered need not always be a nice one" (113). These commonalities lead to friendship, and Lewis further explains that "you can become a man's Friend without knowing or caring whether he is married or single or how he earns his living" (102). Sharing a common interest is the basis of friendship, and this commonality leads to communities of friends. Small communities enjoy getting to know new people and learning new things about each other; the blogosphere is the same way. Rebecca Mead explains that "reading blogs can feel a lot like listening in on a conversation among a group of friends who all know each other really well. Blogging, it turns out, is the CB radio of the Dave Eggers generation" (Perseus Publishing Editors 50). Not only do blogs have the feel of a CB radio from the listening in on conversations aspect, but many times bloggers will have a "handle" or nickname that they use on their blog to help maintain their anonymity. The listening in that Mead discusses can also lead to conversations among the commenters and the sharing of many opinions and ideas. Sometimes the person outside the group joining in may have the freshest opinion and solution. Blogs help to pull a community together to help all of its members. Thus it is possible, and likely, that people will develop friendships in cyberspace, especially in a public space, such as a personal blog.

The commonality of interests mentioned in the previous paragraph is an important factor in friendships and connections in the blogosphere The personal blog provides the perfect platform to give voice to ideas. This idea can be a funny story, a question, or an observation which may be of interest to blog readers or a topic which the blogger wants feedback on. The personal blog is also a place where one can gain more knowledge to be shared with others, and can learn from others about areas of similar interests.

One commonality comes from the expectations or plans which others have for an individual's life, sometimes even before the individual is born. "We all begin life inserted into narratives, stories, and webs that were spun before us, and that will accompany us, and against which more often than not we will have to struggle" (Benhabib 113). This struggle, which is common among people, is a form of presupposition or "horizon" that each individual is born into. "For Hannah Arendt, the 'web' of human relationships and enacted stories constitutes the horizon, in the phenomenological sense, of human affairs. Every speaking and acting human person finds such a horizon as the always already present background from which life unfolds" (Benhabib 112). The fact that each individual has predisposed expectations or a horizon set for them leads to a sense of commonality, and this commonality is the basis of friendship. Lewis writes that "even if the common ground of the Friendship is nothing more momentous than stamp-collecting, the circle rightly and inevitably ignores the views of the millions who think it a silly occupation and of the thousands who have merely dabbled in it" (116). Friendships based on Lewis' understanding lend themselves to the blogo- sphere and the interest-specific blogs which have emerged over time. These personal blogs may discuss a specific hobby (e.g., knitting) or be about a specific life experience (e.g., mommy blogs) but the readers have an interest in the subject or they would not continue to read the blog. This commonality leads to friendship and, although Lewis claims that "a few years' difference in the dates of our births, a few more miles between certain houses, the choice of one university instead of another, posting to different regiments, the accident of a topic being raised or not raised at a first meeting—any of these chances might have kept us apart" (126), the Internet, and the blogo- sphere, have managed to remove many, if not all, of these barriers to friend- ship.

The removal of barriers also creates greater visibility for what is written and shared on the Internet. Our most intimate writings may now be shared with the Internet and those writing may receive responses; these responses help to form a network and may provide the opportunity to realize that the writer is not alone in his or her feelings providing a sense of community and a sense of belonging that cannot be found without sharing those feelings. When ideas have visibility, those ideas take on a life that allows them to grow and flourish in ways that would not be possible without the ideas being available for public consumption. However, this visibility can also lead to personal and societal conflict. From the first blog, people have struggled with what should and should not be visible to others. Justin Hall wrote one of the first personal blogs, which included intimate details of his life. His "actions said, *I'm doing this because I can do it*. They also said, *Soon, everyone will be doing it. . . .* That wasn't what technology was for. Most people don't want to expose themselves fully to the world" (Rosenberg 36). Or do they? The question becomes, why do people share private and intimate information on the Internet, and is this what technology is ideally for?

Did technology create the struggle between public and private? Not real- ly. Arendt and others have always struggled with this issue. The Internet did not create this awareness, it "just made the process of drawing this line more nettlesome. In the end we're each going to find the compromise between sharing and discretion that's right for ourselves" (Rosenberg 44). The deli- cate balance between self and world or public and private suddenly becomes a personal decision as to what should and will be shared with others and what should be kept to ourselves. The visibility which the Internet provides and encourages needs to be tempered by personal decisions. According to Ser- faty, personal blogs "precisely merge public and private spaces in creative ways" and they "represent a way of turning oneself into the hero of one's own life, seen as a work of art and an ongoing creation" (46). Turning one's life into a work of art did not arise with personal blogging, but began with self-representational writing in every form.

Blogs are also a means of self-awareness. By writing ideas and thoughts down, clarity may come to the author even before there is any input from the audience. "Blogs help break through the anonymity and isolation of modern life. They give people a voice and a forum with which to speak truth to power—or at least to reach out and touch someone. . . .pluck from the indifference of daily life a bit of validation for themselves, their ideas, and their creative abilities" (Kline and Burnstein 247–248). Blogs provide a way for people to connect in an over-scheduled and sensory-overloaded world.

Blogs provide a means for self-expression. However, whether the blog is large or small, a dedicated reader base will follow the blog as long as the blogger keeps writing. If the blogger does not post regularly, the readers will move on to other blogs and not return. Unlike most self-representational writing, a blog requires that the writer be consistent and interesting when he or she chooses to write.

Blogs are a form of self-publishing media. Anyone can start a blog. All that is required is an Internet connection, even if that connection is at a public library. The ability to self-publish provides anyone with something to say the ability to say it, without a barrier. According to Bruns and Jacobs, "a key attraction to the blogosphere is, and remains, the potential for individual and informal expression and ungatekept self-publishing . . . and it seems safe to assume that in any future developments of blogging genres, this form of user-led content production, or produsage, will continue to play a significant role" (250).

Without an editor or publisher, the blogger can truly say exactly what he or she wants to say without worrying about edits or revisions changing the true meaning of the statement. This desire to self-publish is innate. According to Kline and Burnstein "our biological and cultural DNA causes us to want to articulate an idea or a vision and 'publish' it, thereby taking ownership of it and credit for it" (xvii). The blog allows its writer to share information with others permanently; once something is on the Internet, it is there forever.

The information shared on a personal blog is almost exclusively nonfiction. Personal blogs are about things that interest and influence the blogger. Diaries, and self-representational writing as a genre, are primarily nonfiction and share observations or opinions of the writer. According to Joe Clark, "a blog is a form of exteriorized psychology. It's a part of you, or of your psyche; while a titanium hip joint or a pacemaker might bring technology *inside* the corporeal you, a weblog uses technology to bring the psychological you *outside* of it" (Perseus Publishing Editors 68). A blog is a technological extension of the blogger; it is another venue for sharing ideas, experiences, and opinions with friends, family, and even strangers. However, if the stranger reads a blog long enough, he or she may become a friend—albeit an online friend.

Blogs are just the latest form of storytelling. They continue a tradition which reaches back to antiquity, but blogs take it beyond what the ancients could have ever imagined. Oral storytelling, as well as written storytelling, has existed as long as man has been able to talk and write. Arendt "thought that storytelling opens up the possibility of different interpretations, based on the differing world views of those who hear the story, and also the possibility of an open-ended, perhaps inconclusive debate about the meaning of the story" (Swift 4). This debate can now occur directly under the story, or post, on a blog. By sharing stories on a blog, people can get feedback and have others share similar stories with the original poster.

One problem with sharing is that some people do not know how much is too much. The biggest complaint with personal blogging, in particular, and the Internet, in general, is people sharing too much information with the world. Oversharing has become a problem offline also. People now talk about subjects that at one time, not that long ago, were considered taboo. The presumed security due to the size of the Internet has allowed people to feel secure sharing information because they erroneously believe that the people they do not want to see it will never be able to find the information on the Internet. This is not always the case. The Internet is large, but information is easy to find if someone knows how to search.

One extreme example of the ability of someone to find information easily occurred in Pakistan. NBC News reports "Malala Yousufzai, the 14-year-old Pakistani girl shot by the Taliban for writing about daily life in the war-torn Swat Valley, was still in critical condition Wednesday after surgery to re-move a bullet" (worldnews). Yousufzai was eleven-years-old when she be-gan her blog, which "chronicled life in the Swat Valley under the brutal and oppressive rule of the local faction of the Pakistani Taliban, who carried out public floggings, hung dead bodies in the streets and banned education for girls" (worldnews). It was this last issue on which Yousufzai was most outspoken. She and her friends believe that they have the right to an educa-tion just like the boys. However, in such an oppressive environment, this right was not a possibility. Yousufzai obviously felt that her blog would not be found by the Taliban; unfortunately, she was mistaken and is now fighting for her life in the United Kingdom. The Internet is not nearly as large as many people believe.

The line between public and private has been blurred. Because the tech-nology exists for individuals to share a lot of information, many individuals may share more information than they originally intend or may believe that the information is private because no one who should not see it knows the address to their blog. Blogging provides a platform for sharing stories and information to anyone who wishes to share. Unfortunately, this sharing can sometimes go to extremes. One example of this which pushes the oversharing extreme is Ranjit's HTTP playground. Although it began as a list of offbeat links it also included "a 'lunch server.' Each day, Bhatnagar would carefully record what he'd had for lunch. . . . Although the 'lunch server' was as much a pun as anything else, it foreshadowed a future in which people would use blogs to record all manner of quotidian data points" (Rosenberg 21). Not only does this show the extent of oversharing which has since become rampant, it also plays into one of the biggest stereotypes of personal blogs as "what I had for lunch" blogs. Oversharing is the largest concern with the Internet, as a whole, and personal blogging, specifically.

READERS/RELATIONSHIPS

The reality that a blog has an audience may be overwhelming for a new blogger. If an individual has wanted to publish for a long time or just wants to share his or her thoughts and ideas on any subject, a blog might seem like the perfect place to do it. But, a new blogger must remember that people will read what he or she writes and if the reader does not agree, he or she may provide comments and begin a dialogue about the issue, which may become heated. According to Stefanac, "most blogs, and certainly the most successful, are communities of a kind, where people argue back and forth via posts and comments" (v). This to and fro begins to form a relationship through dialogue, and people can learn about others' opinions on a topic or hear about different experiences with a specific situation that has occurred.

Beginning a conversation allows for a dialogue to develop and for opinions to be shared, thus forming a community and friendships. This was not possible, on a global level, in the past. Blogging has allowed for location to become less of a factor in friendship. And many times, the blogger does not know the age, sex, marital status, etc. of his or her readers, which may allow many of the other barriers to friendship to be minimized. Many bloggers do not care about the age or location of their readers because bloggers are interested in ideas and experiences.

Bloggers put their ideas out on the Internet in order for people to comment on and discuss them. With a blog, people visit because they want to read what the blogger has written and possibly comment on the post. The comment feature allows the blogger and his or her readers to begin to develop a relationship. The relationship aspect is key to starting and maintaining a personal blog. Many individuals outside of the blogosphere do not feel that developing relationships and communities can occur through an online-only connection; ask any blogger and he or she will tell a different story. One blogger, BusyMom, explains to non-bloggers that the people she meets through her blog are "my friends inside the computer." And one of the great things about blogging friends, whom the blogger may never meet in person, is that "two friends delight to be joined by a third, and three by a fourth, if only the newcomer is qualified to become a real friend" (Lewis 92). There can never be too many readers and commenters on a blog. The more people who read, the more opinions shared, and the more interesting the discussion may become, and the more blogs a reader may start to follow (as well as gain more readers for his or her blog). More discussion creates the possibility for more friendships to be established. Each blog is a reflection of the blogger and the community of readers. Many times the blogger comes to know the readers as well as the readers know the blogger, and this knowledge helps the blogger tailor his or her writing style to that of the more frequent and vocal readers.

Readers are important to a blogger. If there are no readers, the blogger is essentially writing for him or herself. The blogger seeks feedback and most bloggers feel that traffic and link statistics are important so that they do not feel that they are not writing for no one. Most readers comment directly on the blog post in order to share their feedback with the blogger and others, thus helping to build a community. It is not only the blog owner who wants to feel a sense of community with others, it is also the blog readers. By posting a comment publicly on a blog, the reader/commenter opens up the possibility for a conversation with other readers of the blog as well as with the blogger.

Blog readers are looking for relationships as much as the blogger is. In fact, Will Wheaton explains that "a good weblog creates a conversation between the author and the reader, regardless of the subject matter of the blog. And the relationship between the author and the reader grows over time, as each takes part in the ongoing conversation that makes up the core of the blog experience" (Kline and Burnstein 259). This conversation allows for the individuals to learn about each other and create a relationship, or friendship, based on their conversation. An example of this can be found in the creation of Pittsburghbloggers.org. According to Woycheck, "The entire Pittsburgh bloggers group that came together to form the website all came out of meeting via our blogs. A tremendous convergence of creative energy to create the website. Most of the organizing was done online before we even met." Woycheck's experience is not unique. Many bloggers collaborate with others online for many different purposes creating the relationships that are sought by bloggers and others.

The reason that blogs have the ability to create relationships and friendships is because a blog represents a person. The blogger is not a creation of a person; he or she is not a created avatar in a fantasy world. To that end, the blog has become a widely understood and shared rhetorical convention; it functions as a site of relative stability.

The blogger is a real person, sharing his or her views on life. Because the blog is about the author's everyday life, he or she feels the need to share details about his or her world, allowing the reader a glimpse into his or her life. The last portion of that statement allows one to understand how readers begin to feel that they know the blogger personally, because the blogger shares details about what is happening as it happens. This allows a glimpse into the life of the blogger that would not be visible without the blog.

However much the blog represents an individual, it is also important for the blogger to keep the blog updated and interesting. One way to keep the blog interesting is to write for a specific audience. Stone explains that "keeping your readers in mind will help you develop a consistent blogging style. In this way, your blog persona becomes a kind of memorable brand that readers will want to visit again and again" (72). Focusing on the audience allows the blogger to stay on topic with his or her blog; it also allows the blogger to maintain a consistent tone to his or her blog. Stone states that the most effective way for a blogger to find his or her "blog voice" is to keep blogging for six months to a year (71). This allows the audience to get to know the blogger and for the blogger to find his or her way through writing. Stefanac explains, "If bloggers want people to pay attention to what they're doing, they ought to think like standup comics—you always want to leave the audience wanting more" (54). Keeping the blog interesting, updated, and consistent will allow the audience to get to know the blogger and will keep the audience coming back to read more. A consistent blog voice allows the true personality of the blogger to shine through his or her writing, providing the opportunity for the readers to know the blogger.

It is no longer considered taboo have met friends through the Internet. Cyberspace is just another place for people to meet. Blogs, multi-user online games, and social networking sites have allowed friendships through the Internet to become almost mainstream. Developing friendships through blogs and social networking sites has become more likely because "these are real people, putting their lives online" (Perseus Publishing Editors 6). For both blogs and social networking sites, the information shared actually happened or is happening to the individual. It is not a virtual world in which a separate persona exists but real events happening to the individual, and forming a friendship is easier when other people are sharing real events happening to them. Blogs are genuine and provide just another place to meet new friends. Serfaty explains that the dialogues created on blogs "may be only marginally significant as far as their internal meaning is concerned, but they nevertheless function as markers of the acknowledgement of other subjectivities. They institute an I-Thou relationship, because even one who talks about nothing is still attempting to reach out to another individual" (69). Bloggers and commenters are online to make connections and develop relationships; therefore, pretending to be someone different would only hinder that possibility. Blogs are genuine, as are the relationships formed through the blogosphere.

The available blogging software, as well as the sense of community developed through the blogosphere, provides several means of creating connections between the blogger and his or her readers, as well as between the blogger and other bloggers. Links are only one aspect of blogging which allows for relationships to be created and communities to be built; through the comments discussed above and this linking ability, the software provides built-in community building features. Commenting begins the conversation; linking to the other's blog extends the relationship. Comments and links begin to form a community of blogs. If someone comments on a blog, it is most likely because of a shared experience or interest regarding something posted on the blog. This shared interest begins to make connections. After all, if someone reads your blog and likes it, they may mention it on their blog which may bring increased traffic to your site because visitors to a blog are likely to check out other blogs which are linked to the first. The common interest that the original blogger shares with the second is most likely the same interest the reader shares; the link provides the reader a place to get more information or opinions on the topic.

Linking creates a bond between bloggers. Most blogrolls are short, providing links to those bloggers that the blog owner wants to be able to return to regularly. The links create an introduction, of sorts, to other blogs that share similar opinions or interests. Blogging began as a way of sharing links to interesting articles or websites; now blogging provides content with links to original sources and has, usually, a sidebar list of other websites that readers may find interesting. Links were an important part of the creation of blogs and remain an important part of the blogosphere. Links create traffic and traffic builds relationships. It is the power of links between blogs which helps to grow the community around a subject.

Two other aspects of blogging that help build community include the contact and notify functions. Contact provides a way, usually email, outside of the blog for a reader to contact the blogger. There may be something outside of the blog post that the reader would like to share with the blogger and instead of posting it in the comments section and possibly moving the topic off track, the reader may hit the "contact" link and share this information with the blogger off of the blog. This feature allows for a one-to-one connection between reader and blogger, especially if the blogger replies. Notify offers a different type of off-the-blog connection. The notify function allows the readers to request an email or text message when a new post has been added to the blog. This allows the reader to keep current with the blog without having to check each day, or more frequently, to see if the blogger has posted. Again, this feature helps to build community through keeping the conversation current and interactive.

Blogs provide a way to share ordinary lives with other people around the world and many are labors of love as most bloggers spend money to keep their blogs up and do not make money from the blog. Blogs may also provide a place for amazing things to happen through the potential for caring that comes from humanity. Blog sites such as caringBridge provide a means for people to keep friends and family updated on a loved one's medical battle without having to take time away from the patient to make phone calls. Other blogs have been set up to raise awareness of issues or to lend support to others in similar situations. "The New Beautiful" provides exercise and weight loss tips from others struggling with their own weight. The blog is not focused on suggestions from celebrities or trainers trying to get readers to buy their services; this blog is run by five or six women who struggle with their own weight and want to share tips and learn from others going through the same struggle. Another site, which has now received international attention and a book deal for the blogger, is Momastery. Momastery is described by the author as "a place to practice living bigger, bolder, and truer on this Earth. It's a place to practice disagreeing with love and respect. It's a place to remember what you already know: that Love Wins and that We Can Do Hard Things." Momastery takes community to a new level. Glennon, the blogger, and her team help to raise money, through donations from readers, for those who need medical equipment or other items to make their life better and sometimes even tolerable. The readers, known as Monkees, create "Love Flash Mobs" in which a story is posted about someone who needs help and, from donations totaling no more than twenty-five dollars, a person has managed to buy a handicapped accessible van for a woman within five hours. This blog community reaches out to help others and, in the process, manages to help themselves. These blogs, and many others like them, are truly labors of love.

Whether a blog is about a personal life or a labor of love, updates are important to keep readers coming back. If people have an outlet for their opinions or interests, they will use it. According to Rosenberg, "you can't make people shut up they will find a way to say what they want to, if they really need to that's what's wonderful about the internet they can say it, and you don't have to read it" (29). Just because a blogger updates does not mean that every reader will read the update. The benefit of the blogosphere is that readers can decide if and when they read a blog; there is no guilt or pressure that might be felt from an unread email or unopened letter.

Another benefit to the frequency of blog updates comes from the fact that bloggers may be ahead of the mainstream media. Updating as events are unfolding is a benefit that even "breaking news" cannot provide, especially since personal blogs usually involve first-hand accounts of the situation. An example of this occurred on September 11, 2001. "Television, print, and major news sites couldn't keep up with the thousands of bloggers doing original reporting, digging up links to quality information online, and adding their own voice and commentary to what was happening" (Stone 38). Many of the bloggers also lived through the attacks in New York and Washington D.C. and could provide up-to-the-minute accounts of what was happening. Good blogs, and those with the most followers, are updated frequently, if not daily, and provide interesting content for the readers to see and to share with others.

EVOLUTION

The evolution of blogging has happened quickly and has personalized and revolutionized the way people communicate and the way people get their news. Grossman and Hamilton bring the evolution to light: "blogs have gone from an obscure and, frankly, somewhat nerdy fad to a genuine alternative to mainstream news outlets, a shadow media empire that is rivaling networks and newspapers in power and influence" (Kline and Burnstein 363). From a list of hyperlinks to share new webpages to a form of media, blogs have come a long way.

Along the way, personal blogs have settled in to a pattern of everydayness with updates about normal life. Personal blogs have also created niche factions allowing for blogs about knitting, cars, and many other topics to gain momentum. Mommy- and Daddy-blogs are popular ways of sharing stories about kids and asking for advice from parents who have already experienced similar situations. Many different types of personal blogs have emerged, but all personal blogs shine when the personality of the blogger can be felt through the blog. As blogging continues to evolve, personal voice should remain a consistent theme as that is what separates blogs definitively from other forms of mass-mediated communication.

BENEFITS

Reading unknown writers and reading many different viewpoints is one of the biggest benefits of personal blogs. Grossman and Hamilton explain that "blogs showcase some of the smartest, sharpest writing being published. Bloggers are unconstrained by such journalistic conventions as good taste, accountability and objectivity—and that can be a good thing" (Kline and Burnstein 364). Without editors, honesty in writing can come through. Without advertisers, objectivity without concern of alienating someone can be shared. Unabridged and unrestrained sharing of opinions and ideas, i.e., free speech, can happen to large numbers of readers at one time through personal blogs.

Anyone can blog. Blogs allow people to express themselves! Learning about different life situations, finding ways to help those that need help, sharing companionship through a blog can be seen as one of the biggest benefits of all.

FUTURE

Blogging is still in its infancy. It has evolved from a list of links to a personal journal to a media outlet and it will continue to evolve. Looking five, ten, or even fifty years into the future, it is difficult to say with any certainty which path blogging will take, but many technology insiders have opinions. All of these ideas involve blogs remaining in the hands of individuals and not being overtaken by big media conglomerates.

The first venue continues the path of publication for all. Grossman and Hamilton explain that "blogs represent everything the Web was always supposed to be: a mass medium controlled by the masses, in which getting heard depends solely on having something to say and the moxie to say it" (Kline and Burnstein 366). Going back to Berners Lee's vision for his creation, blogging may continue to grow as a means for individuals to share ideas and opinions without fear of censorship or retribution. It could provide a way for individuals to come together for a common purpose.

Closely related to publication is the idea that blogs may slowly find their path into fiction writing. Saffo writes, "I think bloggers may move into the fiction realm, is all I'm saying, since it could be a perfect fit with the wireless technology that's evolving and with people's desire for entertainment" (Kline and Burnstein 340). Tablets and smart phones may push bloggers to share fiction tales with their readers in installments. This has begun in terms of mass media stories already. There are many examples of fan fiction sites on the Internet. These sites provide alternate stories for what is being seen on television or in movies, and many are updated daily with the latest "chapter" of the story. In a sense, these sites are already taking blogging (although they are not called that) into the realm of fiction writing.

Another area which some bloggers are already exploring is that of multimedia publishing. Some bloggers are already creating slideshows of pictures or uploading podcasts of their post so that the readers can listen to the post in the voice of the blogger instead of reading it. The personal media age may create a resurgence of the personal blog as very few social networking sites provide the means to post text, pictures, music, and video to one location and provide a means for only those others who may be interested to provide feedback on a specific work.

Whatever role blogs play in the future, Stefanac is certain of one thing, "whether or not the millions of blogs and related social networks growing up online today will bear fruits as worthy is yet to be seen, but it seems to be an experiment that is worth our time and effort, and perhaps, even our hearts" (33). Blogging began the social networking genre and where it is going can only be imagined, but, like Stefanac, I believe that it is worth pursuing.

NOTES

1. A search for definitive attribution for this statement led to disagreements as to who initially stated it. Weinberger is the most attributed, but even on his blog (hyperorg.com/blogger), many argue that Inus and others may have made the statement first.

Chapter Five

Personal Blogs that Do More

Personal blogs have evolved since their inception. What began as a way for technology insiders to share links, became a way for a person to share the everyday occurrences of their life. Today blogs do so much more.

Today's blogs range from documenting the blogger's day to discussing a particular hobby or cause, to becoming so invested in the community around them that the blogger wants to give something back. Arendt explains that the public realm means doing what is best for the *polis* or community—some bloggers take that definition to heart.

As a community forms around a blog or a cause close to the blogger's heart draws a larger response than other posts on the blog, the blogger may decide to do more, to give back. This chapter will examine three blogs which began as personal pages and have grown into so much more. The blogs that are examined include: CaringBridge, Alice's Bucket List, and Momastery.

CARINGBRIDGE

CaringBridge (http://www.caringbridge.org) was created by Sona Mehring. She writes that she began the site in 1997 when "friends of mine had a premature baby. They asked me to let everyone know what was happening. Instead of making emotional and time draining phone calls, I created a website. In fact, the same night their baby Brighid was born the first Caring-Bridge site was started" (caringbridge.org). CaringBridge became an overnight success by providing comfort and connection to families going through serious medical events and those that wanted to stay informed. If you have ever dealt with a medical emergency in your family, you understand how hard it is to keep everyone up-to-date. CaringBridge allows the family to post one time and provide information to everyone who wants to know.

CaringBridge not only provides an update on the individual's medical condition, but it also provides a common space for family and friends to share their concerns and stories about the individual. CaringBridge provides a community, a public space, for people to send messages, share stories, and support each other, as well as the injured or sick individual.

CaringBridge is free for anyone in need. CaringBridge is supported through donations to the site that continue to make it available to all. Sona Mehring writes that "Almost everyone, right now, knows someone in their life that would benefit from CaringBridge." The site provides a way to "simplify an emotional time"; "have a safe, personal space"; "put support in motion"; and remind everyone that "we're better together" (caringbridge.org). The site allows families and friends to share love and support during one of life's most difficult times. Through their own decisions the family can share as much or as little as they want, balancing the public and private aspects of the healing process.

Several women were willing to share some information regarding their experience on CaringBridge. Maribeth wrote that she had a friend who "had many friends and family around the world. It was difficult for his wife to keep up writing and calling everyone, so CaringBridge was a place she could write things down once, and then people could check in and read the latest." Another friend told a similar story that it was a place for friends and family to get updates on a loved one without causing more anguish to the person responsible for keeping everyone informed. Amy Jo told of a neighbor who found the site as therapeutic for the sick individual as for the family and friends. "When a teenager at the local high school took ill she signed up for CaringBridge. Adults and teenagers used it to check in on what's going on. The teen herself entered her thoughts and feelings directly into the site. It was therapeutic for everyone." The fact that a site started with good intentions is able to continue that for so many others is one of the great public aspects of the Internet.

CaringBridge operates strictly on donations, which allows people who have been helped by the site to give back by supporting it and helping others. Because of one great idea to help tell friends and family about a pre-mature baby, a blog of support and compassion was created and is maintained so that many may benefit from social networking.

ALICE'S BUCKET LIST/ALICE'S ESCAPES

Alice Pyne began her blog in 2011 to share her "Bucket List" of things she wanted to do before she died. Not many fifteen-year-old girls have a "Bucket List" but Alice had terminal cancer and a big heart, she wanted to have fun and help others. Alice was diagnosed with cancer at eleven years old and began her bucket list at fifteen. She lost her battle on January 12, 2013, but her legacy from her "Bucket List" and also from her charity, "Alice's Escapes," live on.

One of the items on Alice's Bucket List was to have everyone who was eligible to become a bone marrow donor to register with a bone marrow organization. The post that mentions this goal went viral and she wrote, "I have managed to get over 40,000 people to join a bone marrow register somewhere in the world." That kind of response is almost unheard of in the blogging world! Her site detailed her daily battle with cancer and the interesting items she was able to complete on her list. Alice had many adventures in her short life. But her desire to help others was her main focus in her life. She continued in her comment that having those donors sign up would "give someone a chance that they might not have got" (alices-escapes.co.uk). When Alice put that item on her list, she knew it would not be able to stop her cancer, but she wanted to help others any way she could.

Alice and her family were given a holiday to spend "a week being looked after by the Torbay Holiday Helper's Network (THHN), based in Devon. All accommodations, food, outings, and activities were given with the compliments of local businesses. After many years of grueling treatments, Alice and her family were able to step back and experience 'normal' family life" (alices-escapes.co.uk). Alice felt so lucky to have this time with her family, she wanted to find a way to help other children who were sick enjoy a holiday with their family. She started Alice's Escapes to do just that.

Alice's Escapes' mission statement reads that the charity wants "to enable every sick child to enjoy a holiday with their family—an escape where they are looked after from start to finish and can simply enjoy spending time together" (alices-escapes.co.uk). Alice's Escapes is made up of a number of businesses that offer free vacations to those families. The holidays that Alice's Escapes provides are in South Cumbria. Before Alice passed away she was able to select a caravan for the charity. The caravan is in Bardsea Leisure Park in Ulveston, UK and provides another location for families to get away and be together. Alice chose the caravan herself and requested that it had some purple decorations in it. Her family is making sure to make that happen. The caravan is called "Mabel's Place" after Alice's faithful Labrador, Mabel. Businesses and individuals help to fund the holidays and Alice's sister, Milly, climbed Mount Kilimanjaro to help raise money for the charity. Alice has left behind a legacy that will, hopefully, continue for years to come providing families with critically ill children some time away from the hospitals and doctors and providing hope for those through increasing the bone marrow donor pool. Alice went out of her way to make society a better place. As Arendt would likely agree, Alice lived for the *polis* helping to make life a little better for others.

MOMASTERY/MONKEE SEE—MONKEE DO

Glennon Doyle Melton got the idea to start her blog, Momastery, after she posted her "25 Things About Me" on Facebook. She was completely honest. She gives this example: "Here was MY #5—5. I am a recovering alcoholic and bulimic. 7 years sober . . . so in many ways I'm actually 7 years old. Sometimes I miss excess booze and food, in the same way you can miss someone who abused you and left you for dead. And here was my best friend's #5—5. My favorite game is Bunco!" As Glennon continues she states that she decided to never go on Facebook again. But, she did. And she was amazed at what she saw. "I saw that my inbox was full. Full of messages from friends and acquaintances thanking me for putting it all out there. . . . And that night I decided to start writing" (momastery.com/blog/2013/02/13/begin-again).

Glennon's story is hers to tell, so I will not even try. This section will discuss Momastery and Monkee See—Monkee Do: the non-profit organization that grew out of Momastery. Monkee See—Monkee Do "is a helping, healing revolution started by a group of women from Momastery in response to a desire for more service projects, more giving and more loving" (monkeeseemonkeedo.org). The community which formed around Momastery had extra energy and love and wanted to help others. This energy created Monkee See—Monkee Do. A small group of women wanted to help others just as Momastery helped them. So they reached out to others who needed help. This was how Monkee See—Monkee Do began.

A phone interview with Amanda Doyle, one of the board members of Monkee See—Monkee Do, provided some information on how the charity got its start. Glennon and Amanda are sisters and they both believe that it is important to do things to help others. Glennon and Amanda personify the public realm. Glennon also believes that when women are filled up they naturally overflow and want to share that goodness with others. The readers at Momastery, the "Monkees," obviously agree. Back in 2009 Glennon received an email asking for help, not for the writer, but for her neighbors who needed help to bring a good Christmas for their family. Glennon agreed to post something on the blog, but offered nothing more as a promise. The post on December 4, 2009 drew thirty comments. According to "Monkee See—Monkee Do" Erin's post set the tone for all of their future projects. "Erin set the tone for our future Holiday Hands projects when she said . . . there is absolutely *no pressure whatsoever at all to participate*. None." And that is how it remains today.

According to Amanda, Glennon lives by this statement from Mother Theresa: "We can do no great things, only small things with great love." Glennon writes with great love and she has the following to prove it. Her readers read for her honesty, her writing, and her love. Glennon is a wonderful person and wonderfully bubbly. Her personality shines through in her writing. She refers to her readers as Monkees because the site is called Momastery. She explains, "We call ourselves Monkees because we're like monks, in that we put our faith in something beyond ourselves, we find value in quiet, and we practice living peacefully in community—here on the internet and beyond. We're unlike monks in that we curse and watch trash tv and become annoyed quite easily" (momastery.com). Not every reader is a mother; in fact, not every reader is a woman—but, every reader is a Monkee!

From the outpouring of love that erupted over Erin's post, Glennon realized that people wanted to help. However, she also realized that some people would be reluctant to help because they could not help much. Therefore, rules were established for giving on Momastery. When Momasatery hosts a "Love Flash Mob" in which Glennon posts about a family or person in need and asks the Monkees for help, she makes sure that everyone feels comfortable getting involved. Here are the rules, as Glennon wrote them:

Love Flash Mob Rules: 1. The Flash Mob will run for 48 hours.[1] After the forty-eight hours are over—the flash mob is closed. Whatever we have at that time is what we have. In the unbelievable event that we raise more than what is needed, the overflow will go to Monkee See—Monkee Do to help other parents in need.
2. THE MAXIMUM DONATION IS $25 dollars. Small things with great love.
3. If you have $5 to give—give it. This is NOT ABOUT THE AMOUNT. It's about the love being offered. Give what you can (UP TO $25) and rest in the fact that YOU ARE MAKING A DIFFERENCE. Changing the world for one mama today. That's a decent day's work. Alright, Lovers of the Light. Let's Make it Rain for this mama. (momstery.com)

And rain it did! A request came in on March 5, 2013, from Sarah. Sarah is the executive director of Project Home Indy. Project Home Indy is a nonprofit agency which helps homeless teen moms in a residential facility. Sarah wrote to Glennon because she had a prospective client in her office that she really wanted to help but had to turn away because they did not have the funding. Glennon asked the Monkees for help. Glennon posted after the Love Flash Mob, "There is no greater honor than participating in the lifting up of another woman. None. Today, you raised 85 thousand dollars in five and a half hours. THAT'S MORE THAN $250 DOLLARS PER MINUTE. I just received a message from Sarah: We called her and told her that it's REALLY going to happen" (momastery.com). Not many other organizations could raise that amount of money in that short of time. However, Glennon allowed the Love Flash Mob to continue because Monkee See—Monkee Do had other women who needed help. The Monkees kept on giving. Sarah provided an update which Glennon shared on June 12: "Just a quick update from

Project Home Indy—your warrior mama has found her first JOB! She is working as a childcare provider in a small daycare. We are SO, SO proud of her" (facebook.com/momastery). Mother Theresa was right, we can do small things with great love, donations of $25 or less helped get this young woman and her child a new start on life.

Out of Momastery and the Love Flash Mobs a charity was formed. In 2009, after the first giving post from Erin, Glennon created Monkee See—Monkee Do. The charity became a 501(c)(3) non-profit in 2013.The charity is run by a board of five volunteers. Except for the necessary fees from the government to keep its non-profit status, all money donated is given to those in need. Glennon believes, as many others may, that the beneficiaries of the giving are not only the receivers, but also the givers. Also, Monkee See—Monkee Do has noticed that many times the givers are actually those who at one point in time were recipients.

Monkee See—Monkee Do has an annual drive around Thanksgiving called "Holiday Hands." This event is like nothing else the charity does. In fact, the charity runs the website and the Monkees do the rest. If someone has a need, they post it on the website. Other Monkees, who want to help, go out to the Holiday Hands page and find a need they can meet. Then they post that they would like to help. It is based on a first come, first served basis. In 2013, "in less than two weeks—the community at Momastery, through Holiday Hands, partnered five hundred families with Monkees across the world. . . . well more than $200,000 in gifts, rent, repairs, and food changed from joyful to grateful hand as a result of the program" (momastery.com). Holiday Hands is one of the biggest projects that Monkee See—Monkee Do does each year.

In 2013, Monkee See—Monkee Do received an email from a Monkee with an unusual request. This Monkee worked for Microsoft and wanted to work with Monkee See—Monkee Do to take on a volunteer project with a school in need. By some twist of fate, there was an email from another Monkee who worked at Battle Monument School in Baltimore, Maryland, who needed help to raise money for technology for her students. Glennon wrote that after she received the email from the teacher, she looked for information on the school. She found out that the school "is a public day school for children between the ages of 3 and 21 with severe and profound mental and physical disabilities." After reading this information, Monkee See—Monkee Do and Microsoft knew that they had found their project. Two thousand Microsoft employees and countless Monkee volunteers took over Battle Monument School. Besides providing the technology through Microsoft, the volunteers redid the landscaping, built a home for the mama duck that takes up home every year to raise her chicks, created an apartment for the older students to learn basic life skills, and upgraded the teacher and staff lounge to give something back to the amazing teachers that gave so much. During our telephone interview, Amanda told me that Microsoft and Monkee

See—Monkee Do are working together again this year to help another school for special needs children. With great love, we can do great things . . . so said Mother Theresa and so live Glennon and the board members at Monkee See—Monkee Do. Their work goes above and beyond what Arendt would consider "doing what is best for the *polis*," they are doing what is right for the world.

These three individuals, Sona, Alice, and Glennon started their blogs as a personal outlet; they have grown to be so much more. Each of their sites has touched so many lives in positive ways and each site continues to do wonderful things for the community, and the world at large. Arendt would understand the need of these women to reach out and help others, after all that was what the public sphere was all about. By opening their hearts and the hearts of their readers, their communities, each woman has created an amazing community and an amazing legacy of helping others through difficult situations and providing a little comfort in the eye of the storm.

NOTES

1. Not all Love Flash Mobs run for 48 hours, but they all have a set time for participation.

Chapter Six

Using Arendt to Navigate the Future of Communication Technology

The relation between Hannah Arendt's philosophy and personal blogs begins a journey of expanding the application of Arendt's understanding of public, private, and social into the era of social media and beyond. By utilizing Arendt's understanding of these realms we can gain a better understanding of the global world in which social media and other interpersonal mediated communication play a large role. Arendt helps us to move our understanding of this "new" world to a much deeper level.

The role of communication technology in interpersonal communication will only intensify as more individuals begin to use social networking and the Internet. Current and future generations will grow up with more access to information and the ability to share more with others than any previous generation. This information overload will affect interpersonal communication to an extent that has yet to be experienced; however, because these future generations will be born into a communication glut, it will not appear as an overload of information or an invasion of privacy to them. Unless there is a turn which reinstates the need for privacy and a general desire not to live a completely mediated social life, as social networking allows, future generations will share anything and everything with anyone, creating a form of the social realm which concerned Arendt.

Although Arendt may not have imagined the technology of the Internet, her research lends itself easily to an examination of the medium. Arendt's concern with the social was that it was consuming the private and the public and making them indistinguishable from each other. Personal blogging, although available to all, does not fit into the realm of the social, but within the public realm, because the blog author and readers have a shared interest in the topic which the blog addresses. However, as interpersonal technology moves forward and more and more people choose to engage in sharing information through social networking sites and personal blogs, the blurring of the public and social may become greater.

Reexamining Arendt's public, private, and social in terms of today's technological world begins our journey. As time evolves, so too does the overall understanding of the meaning of specific terms. For Arendt, the private realm was that which would not be shared with others; it evolved to include the family or very close confidantes; today, the private is truly the realm of the intimate or body. The public, for Arendt, meant the *polis* or community. Doing for the *polis* meant doing what was best for the community at large. In today's technological world, that community could be a virtually known community and, therefore, the members of the community do not need to live in close proximity to one another, but need to share the same common goals for the community and share common interests. For Arendt, the social was "one superhuman family" (*Human* 29).

Today the social includes anyone and everyone connected to the Internet. The understanding of each of these terms has evolved to coincide with the changes in the way humans live and communicate with each other. The most consistent of these terms is public because to Arendt, and today, public means living with others outside of the household. The public is the realm for people to demonstrate their uniqueness and individuality, to stand out from others while, at the same time, fitting in and working toward a common goal. This common goal remains—do what is best for the community and not what is best for the individual. The goal of the public is to make life better for the community as a whole.

Arendt had many concerns with the growth of mass society and the creation of the social realm. For Arendt, the social realm created a loss of freedoms for people; because the social created a sense of belonging by going along with the majority, Arendt feared that the social realm would cause people to give up many of their freedoms in order to "fit in" with everyone else. It was this type of behavior that Arendt witnessed first-hand with the Nazis and that created a lifelong disdain for following the crowd without thought or reflection.

In order to apply Arendt's philosophy fruitfully to today's information-rich society, some liberties must be taken. The use of the evolved meaning of the terms is the first liberty. Utilizing Arendt's philosophy to examine a type of world in which she did not fully anticipate is the second. And, finally, the liberty to apply her philosophy to communication technologies and an ever-changing technological world must be taken. A careful and deliberate reading of her work allows for it to be applied to today's ever-changing world. Arendt herself stated that anything that was put into writing must be let go and observed to determine how others might use it (*Human* xx). It is this kind of forward thinking that allows us to apply her work to all communication technology, specifically personal blogging.

Another aspect of Arendt's work that should be examined in terms of personal blogging is that of storytelling. Arendt believed that storytelling was more focused on human experience than philosophy. It is the aspect of story-telling which makes personal blogs worth reading, and worth visiting again and again. The blog tells a story, the story of everyday life for an individual. This story resonates with readers because they may have experienced similar events, they may find the story amusing or touching, and/or they may share a common interest in what the blogger writes about. Arendt's interest in story-telling may be applied and utilized to gain a better understanding of why someone may start a personal blog.

Simon Swift, in *Hannah Arendt*, examines Arendt's interest in storytell-ing and explains how it helped to move the idea of the public and her understanding of community to a deeper level. Swift explains:

> Story telling proved to be particularly enabling in her attempt to understand events that take place at the limits of what can be understood. . . . Storytelling, as cultural anthropologists have long recognised, is also traditionally the way in which cultures order their understanding of themselves; by being put into the form of a narrative, a series of events can be understood, and so it can be communicated to a wider audience and remembered by the community. If stories help us to understand, if they make events intelligible, they also presup-pose an idea of community inherent in the act of telling, which involves at once the teller of the story, the hero of the action, and the listener or reader who stands back, judges it and responds to it. In this sense, too, storytelling already describes another key idea of Arendt's thought: that free thinking is an activity that can only really go on in the presence of others, in a community, rather than in the quiet withdrawal and meditation demanded by theory. (6–7)

Arendt believed that storytelling helped to focus on the human experience and grow community. After all, the best way to share experiences with others and with future generations would be to tell a memorable story so that it could be shared with others.

In order to move forward in this research some modifications must be made to Arendt's philosophy in order to apply it to interpersonal communi-cation technologies. For this purpose we will use the understanding of the private realm as intimate; we will take the public realm to mean community; and the social realm will still be applied as "one superhuman family" (Arendt, *Human* 29) in which oversharing may become normal and accepted behavior. Through an in-depth reading of Arendt, these interpretations are not altering Arendt's terms, but adapting them to the twenty-first century.

Although social media networks, such as Facebook and Google+, have emerged as the chosen form of interpersonal mediated communication for many, personal blogs portray the dichotomy between public and private more clearly. As was mentioned in chapter 4, bloggers form a community. This community comes together due to similar interests and/or life experiences. The individuals may not live in the same city, state, or even country, but they have similar interests and can connect through the Internet and personal blogs to share their interests with others or, in the case of a personal blog about someone's life, to share stories and experiences with each other, possibly even offering suggestions or solutions to a problem. Blogger Christy Swin explains: "I have to say that I chat with people who have much different views than mine and find it refreshing. We all seem to be on equal footing. No one cares too much about age, socio-economics and other things that could get in the way of a friend. We all just seem to be people who care, at least about a lot of the same things." Many times these online connections can lead to face-to-face meetings, phone calls or private emails with others whom the blogger or reader may never have the opportunity to meet otherwise. Much like the salons during World War II, the blog allows people from many different walks of life to share ideas without being judged for their financial, political, or societal status.

As with any community, the members have guidelines about what information they will and will not share with other members of the community. Serfaty explains the need to keep some things private: bloggers are "highly aware of the public nature of their writings and they accordingly construct a narrative that has very little to do with their inner being" (32). By maintaining some form of boundary regarding what a blogger will share and what he or she will keep private, blogs allow a community to form where oversharing is not the norm, but the exception. Liberty, a blogger, explains that private details are shared through other media if there is a closer relationship between a blogger and a reader, but most of the time the blog does not share private details with everyone who reads it:

> We may only update each other through our Blogs or email or IM, but we try to stay in touch and keep up to date with each other's lives. Even if a friendship has not developed into a face to face relationship, it may still be with someone to whom I confide deepest fears, hopes, dreams and goals or might ask for help or offer assistance in the ways I could if I felt they were in need.

These friendships may originate through a person's blog, but his or her blog is not where the private details and struggles of life are shared. Those details are reserved for close friends or family. Although the blogging genre may have invented oversharing, most personal bloggers have a definite boundary as to what they will or will not share on their blog.

Oversharing can be uncomfortable for the person who shared too much, but most especially for the people the information was shared with. Many times, the information which is shared may be intimate details regarding the blogger's life, making his or her life shallow by living only in public (Arendt, *Human*), but the readers may not know how to respond or deal with the information shared. By having personal boundaries regarding what to share and what not to share, bloggers can minimize the possibility of oversharing. Petronio and others have established the Boundary Management theory so that these personal guidelines can be analyzed and used to help establish boundaries for others.

One benefit of social media, especially blogging, is that those people can have an opinion but only people who want to hear it will visit the blog and read it. By posting this information on his or her blog, the blogger may find others who agree with him or her and therefore will have an outlet for boasting. As a genre which has overcome hostility and abuse (Perseus Publishing Editors 22), personal blogs are a medium where narcissism may be accepted because the blog's readers probably agree with the blogger.

The possibility of collaboration can be seen as one of the great benefits of blogging. Any type of idea or post may encourage others to share their thoughts on a topic. These thoughts may lead to a solution or they may lead to a collaboration of the orginal blogger and the reader; it may even lead to a collaborative effort among several people. Collaboration through personal blog—what a wonderful use of technology. Imagine using this collaboration for a scholarly work—to be able to work with colleagues from around the globe almost instantaneously. The possibilities are endless. A scholar from England would be able to collaborate with a scholar from China and another from the United States and the intellectual material that could be produced due to this collaboration would be unprecedented and would possibly move the area of study forward at a faster rate than ever before.

The comment feature, which almost all bloggers enable when setting up their blogs, allows for the reader and blogger to engage in a conversation, or dialogue, about the topic of the original post. Because more than one person may comment on a post, there is also the possibility that the dialogue could grow to include others. Other than collaboration, this dialogue provides an outlet for people to share stories or make a connection while having a personal connection with the blogger and other readers which allows for the conversation to grow larger than it may offline.

Another benefit of personal blogs is that there is no gatekeeper. No one except the blogger can edit what is written and possibly change the intended meaning. The blogger decides what information is shared and which words will be used to share the stories. This lack of a gatekeeper allows for personal blogs to be a more natural form of CMC than others. This allows for the blog posts and comments to take on a conversational tone. Just as with a conversation, anyone can join in with opinions and comments.

Blogging is about sharing ideas, making connections, and interacting with others. Personal blogs allow for people to carry on conversations with anyone anywhere in the world, making the world appear larger because of the number of connections and smaller because of the immediacy of communication. The interaction created through personal blogging creates a sense of community and expands the blogger's circle of contacts to those who read his or her blog, even if they do not always agree with the blogger.

Because blogging provides a community feel to our mediated world, it provides a positive model for navigating the digital world in which we live. The fact that many bloggers have established boundaries regarding what information is shared and what is private provides a good example of how and what to communicate to others. It is the boundaries and the shared interests which place personal blogging in the realm of the public, in terms of community, and not in terms of the social. Personal blogs are about sharing ideas and events that happen in the everydayness of life and discussing these events, as well as other topics, with other people. These other people read the blog because they are interested in the blogger and what he or she communicates.

Unlike some other forms of mediated communication, the blog allows individuals to communicate *with* each other and not *to* each other. The ability for bloggers to read comments posted by others, and potentially comment back, creates a dialogic space where ideas can be exchanged and discussed. Arnett and Arneson state that "interpersonal communication that seeks to confirm the other in diversity and difference works to understand and address the historicality of the communicators and the conversational context" (30). Knowing that the historical moment in which we live involves CMC and all of the benefits and trials that entails, the ability to work within the diversity as opposed to against it can create a more harmonious community for all.

Arnett and Arneson continue: "dialogue is not meant for the ethereal, but for those willing to walk with others through the mud of everyday life" (32). If reading, commenting, and acting on the posts of personal blogs does not demonstrate the willingness to "walk with others through the mud of everyday life," it would be difficult to find a medium which would do so. The blogger looks for advice, suggestions, and friendship to know that he or she is not alone in the everyday minutiae that is life in the twenty-first century.

Writing posts, reading comments, and responding to comments allows the blogger to learn more about him- or herself and about the people who read and comment. Arnett and Arneson state that "we must carve a human future in an era of technology and activities of today's world—a future in which public respect for person, text, and historical moment can still be a guide" (75). This project demonstrates that blogging may provide the first foray into that future. Allowing others to glimpse in through the open window at the blogger's life creates the human experience through the moment necessary to slow down, focus on others, and interact with others on a regular basis.

A focus on the other is always present in personal blogging. A blogger realizes that his or her blog will be read by other people. After a certain amount of time, in which the blogger and reader learn about each other, the blogger may begin to write with a specific person or persons in mind. Many bloggers notice that as they get to know their "regular" readers, their style of writing shifts so that the readers will be comfortable with it. As mentioned in chapter 1, it is almost impossible to write without some audience, even if it is a future self, in mind. Bloggers must also take into account the affect that their writing may have on others. Not only are the readers affected by what is written, but if the blog post is about another person that person may also be affected by it, either in a good or bad way. It is important for bloggers to remember that their writing does impact others.

One of the reasons that personal blogging creates a community feel is that the writing is real. The person behind the screen typing the blog is a real person, there is no one hiding behind an avatar on a personal blog. The blogger is a real person, typing honest posts about stories, news items, problems, and funny moments in real life. Blogs are real. The people behind the blogs are real. The readers are real. The interaction and dialogue are real. There is no virtual persona being used on a personal blog. The reason that personal blogs are written is because the blogger wants to connect with other people who have similar interests or similar life experiences. Blogging is about communication and shared experiences. Blogging does not separate or distance; blogging draws people together through shared stories.

Not only are blogs honest, those that have regular readers are very well written. Bloggers edit, revise, and focus their writing to produce a quality post based on the topic being discussed. If a blogger is sharing a knitting pattern, the post may look completely different than a post from the same blogger sharing a story about something that he or she saw at work or something that his or her kid did that was funny. Bloggers want to tell their story; they want to write good posts. Bloggers want people to read and comment on their posts; otherwise, the blog is just a place to store memories without feedback.

The blogs of today have one thing in common with the original blogs—bloggers still share links of interest with others. Those links may be to other blogs that the person likes to read or they may be to other websites that share information that is of interest to the blogger. These links provide a trail for the readers to follow if they enjoy the first blog and are looking for other blogs that are similar or other websites which share a similar topic. Blogs provide a map through the blogosphere for those who choose to follow the links.

When an event occurs that affects many people, personal blogs may be able to get information out faster than mainstream media. If an event, such as Hurricane Katrina, Superstorm Sandy, or September 11 occurs, it may be reported by bloggers before the news services can get the story out. Because there are no gatekeepers in blogging, there is no need for the editor or producer to approve the content of the story before getting it out to the public. Also, the blogger may be experiencing the event first-hand. If that is the case, the blogger's account of the situation may be more accurate and more heartfelt than the evening news would provide. Hearing the story from someone who is experiencing it allows the event to seem more real and provides a deeper connection to what is happening than hearing the news from a reporter.

As with all public writing, the blogger assumes a co-ownership of information with his or her readers. The blogger uses a good faith judgment that the readers will not share what is posted on the blog with anyone that it should not be shared with. This is especially true if the blogger established a password-protected link to the information. Although bloggers understand that what is posted on the Internet is posted for everyone there is still an assumed good faith agreement that the information will not be used in harmful or inappropriate ways, especially with those readers who have developed a relationship with the blogger. An example of this, which is well-known, is that of Heather Armstrong. Heather assumed that anyone who read her blog regularly would not share information posted with her boss. Heather posts under a pseudonym, dooce, and does not mention her place of employment by name. Unfortunately, someone at her place of work found her personal blog and shared something Heather had written with her boss. Heather was fired from her job, even though the name of the company was not mentioned. Because Heather was the first person this happened to, being fired for a personal blog post is termed being "dooced." Trust is an important part of communication—trust that the information shared is between those people that were present; trust that the information will not be shared if asked not to share it; and trust that the other person feels the same way about the conversation. Unfortunately, this does not always occur. Blogging takes the conversation to a global level.

Personal blogging allows people to communicate about shared interests and life experiences. Blogging allows individuals to create their own personal brand. The style of writing and subject of the blog begins to build the brand. The design of the blog, even if it is a standard template, brings in some of the personality of a blogger and allows others to see it. The "About Me" section, which most blogs have, allows for a glimpse of the individual and what he or she perceives as the information that the reader may want to know about the blogger. Blogging is truly about the individual and who he or she is. By designing his or her blog with photos, colors, and layout the blogger places his or her personal stamp on the Internet.

Media brings us back to a time of community and conversation. Paul Levinson states that the more "technological communications media evolve" the more "they tend to increasingly replicate the pre-technological or human communication environments of the real world" (9). Continuing, he explains that "technological communication has attempted to overcome the limitations of space and time that are a part of pre-technological environments" (11). It is these limitations that the Internet has helped to alleviate. The more bells and whistles that are created for technology, Levinson argues, the more that mediated communication appears to revert back to having a face-to-face conversation with someone. Levinson goes on to give examples of the telegraph evolving into the telephone and black and white television adding color, making them more like real life than their predecessors. Likewise, blogging has made communicating via computer more like having a conversation than sending an email. Blogging takes us back to a communal feel to communication. Blogging helps us recreate the dialogue that other CMC has taken away. However, blogging goes one step further and allows that dialogue to become global.

Technology is referred to as the "secondary orality" by Walter Ong (Ong 65). A return back to a culture where conversation and oral storytelling were passed on from generation to generation. Ong explains that:

> Secondary orality generates a sense for groups immeasurably larger than those of primary oral cutlure—McLuhan's "global village." Moreover, before writing, oral folk were group-minded because no feasible alternative had presented itself. In our age of secondary orality, we are group-minded self-consciously and programmatically. The individual feels that he or she, as an individual, must be socially sensitive. Unlike members of a primary oral culture, who are turned outward because they have had little occasion to turn inward, we are turned outward because we have turned inward. (66)

Ong demonstrates that a return to orality is different than the original because humans have looked into themselves and have decided that it was necessary to look outward. Ong is stating that as humans, we must communicate with and be concerned with the welfare of others because, as Aristotle stated, humans are "social animals."

One advantage that the secondary orality has over the first is the global reach that may be achieved. Blogs help to reach a global audience. Jacobs and Rushkoff agree that "given the growth rates and decidedly personal nature of the majority of new blogs, it's probably more significant that blogs represent the current renaissance's version of cross-cultural exchange" (242). Sharing cultural customs and well as learning about cultural diversity in terms of traditions, laws, and political awareness has increased tenfold since the founding of the Internet and has taken on a more personal aspect thanks to blogging. Instead of reading a news story about an event or cultural tradition, personal blogs allow readers to hear first-hand about it. The story of Malala Yousufzai, shared in chapter 4, provides a personal account of what it is like to live under Taliban rule. Although many people around the world have heard about the awful acts of the Taliban, Yousufzai's blog and the media attention it received after her shooting, allowed global citizens to understand what it must be like to live in terror every day. Personal blogs provide a glimpse into an individual's life, the cultural traditions of another country, and the political climate in other parts of the world.

What this research hoped to accomplish was to provide a background into the social media genre and offer some suggestions on how to navigate the digital world of the twenty-first century with eyes wide open and with a deliberate look toward the future of mankind. The Internet provides a way for community to grow through shared links, shared interests, and shared experiences; however, without some navigational tools one could get lost in the links. Getting lost in the links does not enable the conversation to continue or dialogue to happen. As digital citizens, we must make deliberate choices as to which links are followed and what information is shared. Sharing too much, as can easily happen without set boundaries, can lead to a very shallow life lived entirely in public. Arendt understood that both public and private were necessary in order to live a full life; utilizing her philosophy as guideline can enable this and future generations to maintain some aspect of a private life while still navigating the increasingly digital world.

The collaboration set in motion through personal blogging can only grow as more and more individuals get on the information highway. However, each person must use careful and educated judgment as to what information is reliable and which should be examined more closely. The Internet, in general, and blogging, specifically, provides a lot of information and allows information to be found easily, almost too easily. Human beings still need to know facts, history, and traditions and not just know where to look it up. The loss of all traditions and history could occur if the human race relies on technology to store the information. One computer virus could completely erase the memory of the human race; that would be tragic. The links provided through blogs are excellent ways to find and share information with others, but that information needs to be learned and shared in other ways also. Relying on technology to store all memories and facts should never become an option for humanity.

Personal blogs allow people to share information with others, both known and unknown to the blogger. This information begins to tie these individuals together through shared interests or shared experiences. As these ties strengthen, even if the individuals have never met face to face it becomes evident that they are forming a community. As with most communities, it is important to follow Arendt's view of public and do what is best for the community and not for a specific individual. If this mindset can be extended through the blogosphere and eventually through all social media, the world—mediated or not—will become a much better place for everyone.

Through Arendt's understanding of public and social we can make clear distinctions between personal blogging and social networking sites. The first and most important distinction is that a personal blog is built around a specific topic. It is the interest in this topic that draws the blogger and the readers together. This is very different than social networking sites which are more about self-promotion than any concern about community or shared interests/experiences. Social networking sites encourage narcissism and a focus on the individual, whereas personal blogs are about making connections and building community. Blogging invites people to disagree. Bloggers do not post for everyone to agree, but to begin a conversation about the content of the post. This allows for a diversity of opinions and a serious discussion about the issue. Blogging does not discriminate in terms of relationship to the blogger, sex, race, or social status—if the reader has an opinion, it is welcome. With most social networking sites the person must be approved or invited to see an individual's posts.

Personal blogging creates an opportunity for the readers to "know" the blogger. The readers are usually more than casual acquaintances, especially if they have read the blog for a while. Julie Powell, author of *Julie and Julia* acknowledges the relationship that can happen between a reader and a blogger when, in her "Acknowledgments" at the end of the book, she thanks "anyone who ever read my blog, ever ever, but especially all of you who became family to me" (309). The term "family" indicates a bond of some sort. Of course, it would be difficult to create such a deep connection without good storytelling.

Blogs tell stories. The blogger, at least one who can get and maintain an audience, must write well. Readers will point out errors in a blog post. Readers will not continue reading the blog if there are a lot of errors or the posts are poorly written. The blogger must take time to read, revise, and edit each story before posting it to his or her blog. Many readers only know the blogger through what he or she posts so if the blogger expects people to take him or her seriously then he or she must take the time to proofread, edit, and revise a post before sending it to the blog. Quality writing is important in the blogosphere because that is the first impression that a reader has of the blogger. Arendt discusses the importance of storytelling in her work, stating that it is better at explaining the human experience than philosophy. If the story is to be memorable, it must be well written.

Another difference between personal blogs and social networking sites is the format. A blog has a specific format with the latest entry placed at the top of the page; this is similar with social networking sites. However, the social

networking site also posts other users' entries on the same page. These entries may or may not be related to the individual's post—they may be photos,
cartoons, reposts of another person's entry, etc. With the blog, the posts are
all from the same person and the comments are available only after opening a
link. This allows the blog to maintain a cleaner experience where only the
posts by the blogger are available on the main page. The continuity of content provides another distinction between the publicness of the blog—stick-
ing to one topic and allowing others to provide insight, and the socialness of
social networking—sharing everything that is remotely connected to the
user.

Arendt provides the ground from which this examination of personal
blogs begins. This project is the beginning of further research in the examination of the public, private, and social realms regarding interpersonal communication and CMC. Applying Arendt's work to our mediated world allows us
to gain a deeper understanding of how CMC has changed the way we communicate and how to make informed decisions about what to communicate
with others, and which others to communicate with.

Works Cited

AFL-CIO. http://www.aflcio.org. Accessed: April 2012. Web.

Alice's Bucket List. alicepyne.blogspot.com. Web.

Alice's Escapes. alices-escapes.co.uk. Web.

Anderson, Rob, Kenneth N. Cissna, and Ronald C. Arnett, eds. *The Reach of Dialogue: Confirmation, Voice, and Community.* Cresskill, NJ: Hampton Press, 1994. Print.

Arendt, Hannah. *The Human Condition.* Chicago: University of Chicago Press, 1998. Print.

———. *The Origins of Totalitarianism.* New York: Harvest Books, 1994. Print.

———. *Rahel Varnhagen: The Life of Jewish Woman.* San Diego: Harvest Books, 1974. Print.

Arnett, Ronald C. and Pat Arneson. *Dialogic Civility in a Cynical Age: Community, Hope, and Interpersonal Relationships.* New York: State University of New York Press. 1999. Print.

Aristotle. *Politics.* New York: E. P. Dutton & Co., 2004. eBook.

Baehr, Peter, ed. The Portable Hannah Arendt. New York: Penguin Books, 2000. Print.

Bahktin, M. M. *Art and Answerability.* Eds. Michael Holquist and Vadim Liapunov. Trans. Vadim Liapunov. Austin: University of Texas Press. 1990. Print.

Benhabib, Seyla. *The Reluctant Modernism of Hannah Arendt.* Thousand Oaks, CA: SAGE Publications. 1996. Print.

Bick, Jonathan. *101 Things You Need to Know About Internet Law.* New York: Random House, 2000. Print.

Bruns, Axel and Joanne Jacobs, eds. *Uses of Blogs.* New York: Peter Lang Publishing, Inc, 2006. Print.

CaringBridge. Caringbridge.org. 2013. Web.

Carr, Nicholas. *The Shallows: What the Internet Is Doing to Our Brains.* New York: Norton. 2006. eBook.

Chesebro, James W. and Donald G. Bonsall. *Computer-Mediated Communication: Human Relationships in a Computerized World.* 1989. Tuscaloosa, AL: University of Alabama Press. Print.

Farrell, Thomas B. "On the Disappearance of the Rhetorical Aura." *Western Journal of Communication,* 57 (Spring 1993): 147–158. Web.

Frank, Anne. *The Diary of a Young Girl.* New York: Bantam Books, 1986, Print.

Gunter, Barrie. "Blogging—Private Becomes Public and Public Becomes Personalised." *Aslib Proceedings: New Information Perspecitves.* 61.2 (2009): 120–126. Web.

Horton, Donald and R. Richard Wohl. "Mass Communication and Para-Social Interaction: Observations on Intimacy at a Distance." *Particip@tions.* 3.1 (2006). Web.

Johnson, Alexandra. Leaving a Trace: On Keeping a Journal. New York: Back Bay Books, 2009. Ebook.

Kagle, Steven E. *American Diary Literature 1620–1799*. Boston: Twayne Publishers, 1979. Print.

———. *Early Nineteenth-Century American Diary Literature*. Boston: Twayne Publishers, 1986. Print.

———. *Late Nineteenth-Century American Diary Literature*. Boston: Twayne Publishers, 1988 Print.

Kline, David and Dan Burstein, eds. *Blog! How the Newest Media Revolution is Changing Politics, Business, and Culture*. New York: Squibnocket Partners, LLC, 2005. Print.

Lasch, Christopher. *The Culture of Narcissism: American Life in an Age of Diminishing Expectations*. New York: W. W. Norton & Company, Inc, 1979. Print.

Lenhart, Amanda and Susannah Fox. "Bloggers: A Portrait of the Internet's New Storytellers". Pew Internet and American Life Project. Washington, DC: Pew. (2006). Web.

Levinson, Paul. *Human Replay: A Theory of the Evolution of Media*. New York University: University Microfilms International. 1979, Print.

———. *New New Media*. Boston: Allyn & Bacon, 2009. Print.

Lewis, C. S. "Friendship" pp. 87–127. *The Four Loves*. New York: Harcourt, Brace & World, Inc, 1960. Print.

Marx, Karl. *The Eighteenth Brumaire of Louis Bonaparte*. Marxists.org/archives/marx/works/download/pdf/18th-Brumaire.pdf. Accessed March 2014. Web.

McLuhan, Marshall. *Understanding Media: The Extensions of Man*. New York: McGraw-Hill. 1964. Print.

Meyrowitz, Joshua. "The Separation of Social Place from Physical Place." *The Reach of Dialogue: Confirmation, Voice, and Community*. New Jersey: Hampton Press, 1994. Print.

———. *No Sense of Place: The Impact of Electronic Media on Social Behavior*. New York: Oxford University Press, 1986. eBook.

Miller, Carolyn R. and Dawn Shepherd. "Blogging as Social Action: A Genre Analysis of the Weblog." *Into the Blogosphere: Rhetoric, Community, and Culture of Weblogs*. (retrieved Proquest, Duquesne University, August 2007). Web.

Momastery. momastery.com/blog/. Web.

Monkee See Monkee Do. monkeeseemonkeedo.org. Web.

Nardi, Bonnie A., Diane J. Schiano, Michelle Gumbrecht, and Luke Swartz. "Why We Blog." *Communications of the ACM*. 47.12 (2004): 41–46. Web.

Ong, Walter. "Orality, Literacy, and Modern Media." In David Crowley and Paul Heyer. *Communication in History: Technology Culture, Society*. Third Edition. New York: Longman, 1999, pp.60–67. Web.

Øverenget, Einar, "Heidegger and Arendt: Against the Imperialism of Privacy." *Philosophy Today* 39:4 (1995): 430–444. Web.

Parks, Malcolm R. and Kory Floyd. "Making Friends in Cyberspace." *Journal of Communication*. Winter 1996; 46, 1; ABI/INFORM Global. Pg. 80.

Perseus Publishing Editors. *We've Got Blog: How Weblogs are Changing Our Culture*. Cambridge, MA: Perseus Publishing, 2002. Print.

Peters, John Durham. *Speaking into the Air: A History of the Idea of Communication*. Chicago: The University of Chicago Press, 1999. Print.

Petronio, Sandra. *Boundaries of Privacy: Dialectics of Disclosure*. Albany, NY: State University of New York Press, 2002. Print.

———. "Road to Developing Communication Privacy Management Theory: Narrative in rogress, Please Stand By." *The Journal of Family Communication*. 4.3 & 4 (2004). 193–207. Web.

———. "Translational Research Endeavors and the Practices of Communication Privacy anagement." *Journal of Applied Communication Research*. 35.3 (2007). 218–222. Web.

Pitkin, Hanna Fenichel. *The Attack of the Blob: Hannah Arendt's Concept of the Social*. Chicago: The University of Chicago Press, 1998. Print.

Plato. *Phaedrus*. Walter Hamilton, trans. London: Penguin Books, 1988. Print.

———. *The Republic*. Trans. Benjamin Jowett. Mineola, NY: Dover Publishing, 2000. eReader.

Powell, Julie. *Julie & Julia: My Year of Cooking Dangerously*. New York: Back Bay Books, 2005. Print.

Ramsey, Eric. "Suffering Wonder: Wooing and Courting in the Public Sphere."*Communication Theory*. 8:4 (November 1998): 455–475. Web.

Reeves, Byron and Clifford Nass. *The Media Equation: How People Treat Computers, Television, and New Media Like Real People and Places*. Cambridge: Cambridge University Press, 1998. Print.

Ringmar, Erik. *A Blogger's Manifesto: Free Speech and Censorship in a Digital World*. London: Anthem Press, 2007. Print.

Rosenberg, Scott. *Say Everything: How Blogging Began, What It's Becoming, and Why It Matters*. New York: Crown Publishers, 2010. eBook.

Serfaty, Viviane. *The Mirror and the Veil: An Overview of American Online Diaries and Blogs*. Amsterdam: Rodopi B. V. 2004, Print.

Shirky, Clay. *Here Comes Everybody: The Power of Organizing Without Organizations*. New York: Penguin Press. 2008, Print.

Stefanac, Suzanne. *Dispatches from Blogistan: A Travel Guide for the Modern Blogger*. Berkeley, CA: New Riders. 2007, Print.

Stark, Andrew. *Drawing the Line: Public and Private in America*. Washigton, DC: The Brookings Institution. 2010, Print.

Stone, Biz. *Who Let the Blogs Out*. St. Martin's Press. New York, 2004. Print.

Swift, Simon. *Hannah Arendt*. New York: Routledge, 2009. Print.

Turkle, Sherry. *Alone Together: Why We Expect More from Technology and Less From Each Other*. New York: Basic Books,2011. eBook.

Twenge, Jean M. and W. Keith Campbell. *The Narcissism Epidemic: Living in the Age of Entitlement*. New York: Free Press,2009. Print.

Walker Rettberg, Jill. *Blogging: Digital Media and Society Series*. Malden, MA: Polity Press, 2008. Print.

Walther, Joseph B. "Computer-mediated Communication: Impersonal, Interpersonal, and Hyperpersonal Interaction." Communication Research. 23:1 (1996): 3–43. Web.

World News. Worldnews.nbcnews.com. Accessed October 2012. Web.

Index

Alice's Bucket List / Alice's Escapes, 71, 72, 73, 77

Arendt, Hannah, 2, 3, 15, 16, 17, 19, 20, 22, 25, 26, 27, 29, 30, 32, 33, 34, 35, 36, 37, 39, 43, 47, 50, 51, 55, 57, 59, 60, 62, 71, 73, 77, 79, 80, 81, 83, 88, 89, 90; *Human Condition*, 11, 19, 20, 21, 22, 23, 24, 26, 27, 28, 29, 30, 31, 32, 33, 34, 36, 38, 39, 42, 80, 81; *Origins of Totalitarianism*, 31; *Rahel Varnhagen*, 24, 25, 31, 35, 36, 37

Aristotle, 2, 12, 19, 20, 87

Audience, 1, 2, 4, 5, 6, 7, 12, 13, 16, 17, 27, 35, 36, 38, 40, 41, 48, 56, 57, 60, 61, 63, 65, 79, 81, 85, 87, 89

Bakhtin, 13, 52

Blogger, 8, 9, 10, 11, 12, 13, 14, 15, 16, 17, 34, 36, 47, 48, 50, 51, 55, 56, 57, 58, 59, 61, 63, 64, 65, 66, 67, 68, 69, 70n1, 71, 81, 82, 83, 84, 85, 86, 87, 88, 89, 90. *See also* diarist; writer

Blogging / Blogs, 2, 3, 7, 8, 9, 10, 11, 12, 13, 14, 15, 16, 17, 19, 36, 38, 41, 43, 46, 47, 48, 50, 51, 53, 55, 56, 57, 58, 59, 60, 61, 62, 63, 64, 65, 66, 67, 68, 69, 70n1, 71, 72, 73, 74, 77, 79, 80, 81, 82, 83, 84, 85, 86, 87, 88, 89, 90

Blogosphere, 10, 11, 12, 15, 51, 56, 57, 58, 59, 60, 61, 63, 65, 66, 67, 85, 89

Boundaries / Boundary, 9, 15, 44, 45, 46, 47, 82, 83

Boundary Management Theory, 44, 47, 83

CaringBridge, 71, 72

Communicate / Communication, 1, 2, 9, 10, 12, 13, 14, 16, 19, 25, 27, 29, 35, 36, 37, 38, 39, 40, 41, 42, 43, 44, 45, 46, 47, 48, 49, 50, 51, 52, 53, 68, 79, 80, 81, 84, 85, 86, 87, 90

Communication Privacy Management, 44

Communication Technology, 38, 39, 40, 41, 42, 43, 44, 49, 53, 79, 81

Computer Mediated Communication (CMC), 41, 42, 43, 47, 48

Dialogue, 10, 13, 14, 51, 52, 57, 63, 65, 83, 84, 85, 87, 88

Diaries, 1, 2, 3, 4, 5, 6, 8, 10, 16, 17, 17n1, 36

Diarist, 3, 4, 5, 6, 16, 17. *See also* blogger; writer

Ethics, 15, 39

Frank, Anne, 1, 4

Hall, Justin, 8, 10, 14, 60

Internet, 2, 7, 8, 9, 10, 12, 46, 47, 50, 55, 56, 58, 60, 61, 62, 63, 65, 67, 69, 72, 75, 79, 80, 82, 86, 87, 88
Interpersonal, 12, 16, 37, 39, 40, 41, 43, 44, 47, 48, 49, 50, 51, 79, 81, 84, 90

Journals, 2, 3, 4, 5, 6, 7, 9, 16, 17, 36, 69

Levinson, Paul, 49, 50, 87

Momastery, 67, 71, 74, 75, 76
Monkee See-Monkee Do, 67, 74, 75, 76, 77

Parasocial Framework, 40, 44, 47, 48
Petronio, Sandra, 44, 45, 46, 47, 83
Privacy, 4, 5, 20, 21, 22, 23, 24, 27, 42, 44, 45, 46, 47, 79
Private, 1, 2, 3, 4, 5, 6, 7, 8, 9, 15, 16, 17, 19, 20, 21, 22, 24, 25, 26, 27, 28, 29, 31, 32, 36, 42, 44, 45, 46, 47, 53, 56, 57, 60, 62, 72, 79, 80, 81, 82, 84, 88, 90
Public, 2, 3, 5, 6, 7, 9, 12, 15, 16, 17, 19, 20, 21, 22, 23, 24, 25, 26, 27, 28, 29, 30, 31, 32, 33, 34, 35, 36, 37, 38, 39, 41, 42, 46, 47, 52, 55, 56, 57, 58, 59, 60, 61, 62, 64, 71, 72, 74, 76, 77, 79, 80, 81, 82, 83, 84, 86, 88, 89, 90

Reader, 2, 63, 81, 82, 83, 86
Readers, 4, 8, 9, 10, 11, 13, 14, 17, 36, 39, 50, 57, 58, 59, 60, 63, 64, 65, 66, 67,

68, 69, 74, 75, 77, 79, 81, 83, 85, 86, 87, 89

Self-representational writing, 1, 2, 4, 5, 6, 7, 11, 12, 16, 19, 60, 61
Social, 2, 3, 8, 9, 12, 16, 19, 20, 21, 25, 26, 30, 32, 33, 34, 35, 36, 37, 38, 42, 43, 48, 50, 55, 57, 58, 79, 80, 81, 84, 87, 89, 90
Social Media, 16, 50, 51, 79, 81, 83, 88, 89
Social Networking, 8, 9, 41, 42, 44, 47, 50, 53, 56, 65, 69, 72, 79, 80, 89, 90
Socrates, 1, 20, 39, 41
Story, 2, 6, 11, 12, 27, 28, 30, 56, 57, 59, 62, 63, 67, 69, 72, 74, 81, 85, 86, 88, 89

Technology, 2, 8, 9, 10, 13, 16, 17, 33, 38, 39, 40, 41, 42, 43, 44, 47, 48, 49, 51, 53, 55, 60, 61, 69, 71, 76, 79, 81, 83, 84, 85, 87

Warhol, Andy, 1, 13, 56
Writer, 2, 3, 4, 5, 6, 14, 15, 16, 39, 55, 61, 68, 74. *See also* blogger, diarist
Writing, 1, 2, 3, 4, 5, 6, 7, 8, 11, 12, 13, 14, 16, 17, 19, 31, 39, 43, 46, 50, 56, 60, 61, 62, 63, 64, 65, 68, 69, 72, 74, 80, 82, 84, 85, 86, 87, 89
Written, 3, 6, 9, 10, 12, 15, 24, 36, 40, 41, 62, 75, 83

About the Author

Kristin Roeschenthaler Wolfe is an Instructor of Public Speaking and Rhetoric and Composition at Pennsylvania State University. She completed her PhD in Rhetoric at Duquesne University, in Pittsburgh, after spending thirteen years working in corporate communications, public relations, advertising, and Internet development. She lives in Baden, Pennsylvania, with her husband, Don, and her Border Collie/Lab mix, Soxy.

Leabharlanna Poiblí Chathair Bhaile Átha Cliath
Dublin City Public Libraries